SHE HAD NO REGRETS

The Life of a Girl Who Knew Who She Was

JULIA KAY DUERLER

Pluvial
Press

Any Internet addresses in this book are offered as a resource. They are not intended in any way to be or imply an endorsement by Pluvial Press LLC; nor does Pluvial Press LLC vouch for the content of these sites for the life of this book.

Requests for information should be sent via e-mail to Pluvial Press LLC: PluvialPress@gmail.com.

Photos used with permission by: Stephanie Klemm p. 29, Amy Green p. 65 Linda Lonneman p. 93, Jennifer Snyder (graphic design) p. 216, Brian Egan p. 217, Lisa Russell p. 219. All other photographs by a member of the Duerler family.

Cover photograph, interior drawings, and artwork by Kayla Marie Duerler

Cover and interior design: Harrington Interactive Media (harringtoninteractive.com)

ISBN 978-1-7352500-0-7 (Paperback)
ISBN 978-1-7352500-2-1 (Kindle)
ISBN 978-1-7352500-1-4 (ePub)

Library of Congress Control Number: 2020911206

For Kayla,
You amaze me, child.
I'm so proud of you.
I can't wait to see you again!

For the Class of 2020,
who are well-acquainted with loss,
may you always experience
beauty from ashes.

And for Jeff and Rachel,
who went through the valley of the shadow of death.
There is no one I'd rather walk alongside.
I'm so thankful our love and faith
endures.

Table of Contents

KEY

🟦 Identity

🌐 Place in This World

🔺 Relationships

The categories for the main chapters of this book are based on this statement in Kayla's notes.

3 / 1 / 18   All Teens Deal With

→

finding their identity
finding their place in the world
dealing with family, friends, and enemies
angst / hormones

Foreword from Kayla's Dad

Why should you read this book? If you knew Kayla at all, that's a silly question. Enough of this foreword—let's get on with the book!

But if you didn't know her well, it's a fair question. Perhaps you only know *of* Kayla. Maybe you heard something about what happened and were intrigued by her story. Or someone recommended this book to you. Or you might be following the social media profiles dedicated to her life.

There are three main reasons why you should read this book:

1. Kayla, the subject
2. Julia, the author
3. God, the hero

1. The Subject: Kayla

Anytime a teenager dies, there is an unsettling, collective ache that ripples out both near and far. What happened, and what led up to it? It's natural to wonder. But even more personally, what meaning are we to make of it? How can we find some sense of steadiness living in a broken world where death seems to strike so suddenly and indiscriminately?

If we slow down long enough to let it sink in, an uneasiness grows. Reading about a treasure who *seemed to be* tragically taken from us at sixteen may be the very last thing we want to do. And yet this is different. Reading a memoir of a young woman who lived with no regrets can help us process our bewilderment and discomfort with life in such a shakable world. And, in the end, we can have more of the peaceful resolve that Kayla embodied.

So there's that, and then there's a wonderful comradery that can come from getting close to someone like Kayla. Will you entertain the possibility that it is possible to grow in friendship with someone who is no longer here on earth?

As her father, I continue to be fascinated with her angle on life, her unique style and personality, her aspirations, and, more than anything else, her deep and authentic spirituality. Having a personal relationship with Jesus—that was clearly a fountain of life for Kayla.

Please understand, Julia and I aren't wishfully retrojecting our beliefs onto Kayla's life to make some sense of what feels like a premature death. No, *it's more the reverse.* Thanks to her love of words and books, we have treasure troves of her writings which have opened up a profound spiritual perspective we didn't always know was there. These insights have brought the bright light of hope to the darkest depths of our grieving souls.

Said simply, Kayla's life is inspiring. It just is. Unlike the stereotypical "golden child" who seems to be born with everything going for him or herself, Kayla is relatable. She is more like you and me . . . and yet she is *more*, in many ways, than what I am. And so I find her example stirring within me a deeper hunger for both simple contentment and soaring ambition. We think Kayla's short sixteen years were packed with a lifetime of wisdom, and this book gives you a behind-the-scenes understanding of what made her tick. As you will see, it's not just famous people who make history. The small stuff matters more than any of us realize.

2. The Author: Julia (Known as Julie to Many)

Why would someone who doesn't consider herself a natural writer devote the better part of a year to compiling and writing a work that could open her personal life and family to critique and—even more terrifying—potential indifference about someone so infinitely cherished? Julia made the sacrifice and took the risk because this wasn't a choice for her, it was a calling. Every page of this book has been bathed in prayer, every sentence conceived by total dependence on God.

Kayla's mom, my wife, is the real deal. Everything she writes about, she believes. That kind of authentic faith shaped and molded Kayla's life. Every day Rachel (Kayla's younger sister) and I get to bask in the joyful relief that emanates from Julia's spiritual perspectives. And now you can too.

Thanks to hundreds of providentially preserved moments carefully recorded in a memory book from pregnancy on, you will be reading actual quotes (not just "I-think-the-conversation-went-something-like-this" memories). This kind of detail makes the moments come alive. Julia's willingness to share weakness, struggle, and even "bad mom" moments, not just the wins, welcomes you into our family.

I love reading her straightforward, down-to-earth style that is saturated with substance. There is enough detail to draw you in . . . but not so much that you get lost in the setting without remembering the point.

As you know, it takes a village to raise a child, and Julia is eager to demonstrate the lasting impact made by Kayla's friends, family, teachers, and adult role models. Perhaps that's you, and even more certainly, that *can* be you. Kayla's life, as described from the perspective of her mom and mentor, will encourage you to make a lasting impact on others.

3. The Hero: God

And now, the third and best reason you should read this book. He is the one who gave Kayla her passion. He is the beauty behind her art and expression. He is the freedom heralded by her laughter and whimsy. He is the Creator who activated her many pursuits, and he is the ultimate truth behind every question she wrestled with. He is the best author of the most profound and gripping story ever told, one that you and I are invited into.

Should you find something stirring you to a more purposeful life as you read this book, then God is reaching out to you.

If there is any uncertainty about the meaning of life and what happens when we die . . .

If there is any hint of hunger in you to make the most of whatever time you have remaining . . .

If you need clarity about today and confidence about eternity . . .

. . . then you've got the right book. Begin reading and you will find the pieces of the puzzle start coming together. You may be surprised to discover that, in the end, the picture of Kayla's life has *you* in it.

Jeffrey Duerler, M.Div., Ph.D.
AKA Kayla's Daddy

A Personal Note from Kayla's Mom

I'm weeping as I type this. I literally just pulled myself off the ground from where I collapsed to my knees.

My tears have fallen for loads of reasons as I grieve this tremendous loss, and I even weep for joy at times. But today is different—a first.

I'm crying over this book. I desperately want to communicate who Kayla is in a way that honors her and represents her well, but I'm overwhelmed at the task.

How do I tell you about her? How do I help you understand such a deep, unique, complex, yet darling girl?

Will you get her?

Will you appreciate her?

There were many times I struggled to understand my daughter, yet I adored her to no end. My love for her keeps growing even though she's gone. My eyes, my throat, and my heart are swollen with love, maternal pride, and pain.

God designed Kayla and gave her as a gift, and we tenderly (though not perfectly) raised His child. It will be impossible to fully capture Kayla's spirit inside the pages of this book, so, "Lord, help me do this. May this book glorify You, honor her, and help others."

Deep breath.

Since Kayla's passing, I read several memoirs of precious young lives and my heart wanted to know more. For example, in *Rachel's Tears*, I was intrigued by her journal entries. It was an honor to follow the inner workings of her relationship with God. In *Rare Bird*, I savored the descriptions of sweet Jack's personality. I shared with my husband how Jack maintained a seventy-day dream chart. His intelligent, quirky, methodical ways reminded us of our girl. When I read *Colors of Goodbye*, I wished I could view videos of Katie energetically painting in action as described. And after watching *The Miracle Season* and reading the book, I spent some time appreciating the real Caroline's infectious enthusiasm in YouTube videos.

There's something about cherishing the ones we lose too early, and it means more than words can say when others—even strangers—cherish them also. It somehow helps validate the incalculable loss while it keeps their memory alive. The value of a human life is beyond comprehension, but we sense the significance most intensely when that life is gone. *Each person is irreplaceable—each soul a treasure.*

In light of this, I am offering you the opportunity to know Kayla on a deeper level. For those who have been following on Facebook and Instagram, you will discover even more about our precious girl.

Though her life was brief, Kayla left behind a legacy of writings, journal entries, artwork, and photos. She accomplished more than I could ever include, even though I wish I could share everything! Here are her journals from just the last two years of her life.

This is a pictorial memoir because the more Kayla's writings and drawings do the talking, the better. And trust me, they speak loud and clear.

Throughout these pages, I refer to her memory book. This is a scrapbook journal I was writing before she was born until her eighth-grade year. It is full of little stories about her life that I had planned to share with her when she was an adult.

Also, in various chapters, you'll see "Conversations with Kelsey" set apart from the rest of the chapter. Kelsey was Kayla's Bible study leader. She is a deep and vibrant young woman. Kayla felt comfortable to share candidly with her and their group. Kelsey recalls insightful conversations that help us see how God was working—preparing her soul for eternity—and is now using those conversations to heal us.

I hope that you are blessed, challenged, and inspired as you get to know Kayla and the way she lived her life. With all my heart, I pray that her brief run on earth will spark an eternal flame in you.

> *"Nothing sounds better than living my small life well."*
> — Emily Henry (one of Kayla's favorite quotes)

∞∞∞∞∞

As some have pointed out, Kayla's departure happened on a date with three sideways infinity symbols 8-8-18. I will use these at various points in the book to transition to how the topic relates to you and me.

Introduction

Kayla repeatedly wrote these Latin words in the last months of her life. The mysterious phrase showed up in her journals, on a playing card that she used as a bookmark, in schoolwork, and at the end of videos.

It means *the die is cast.*

The sense of the meaning is "the future is determined, there are no more options, events will proceed in an irreversible manner; the point of no return has been passed."[1]

Then it happened. 8-8-18.

The events proceeded in an irreversible manner.

It was a beautiful summer day. She was heading home with her grandparents after a few hours of enjoyable driving practice. Grandpa, in the front passenger seat, was unfamiliar with that area. He suggested twice that they go the way he knew, but adventurous Kayla, with Grandma's support, followed the GPS directions instead.

---

[1] **Wiktionary.com**

She came to a stop sign at a tricky intersection with limited visibility on a country road. She thought the coast was clear and turned left. Her grandfather shouted, "Kayla, the truck!" The driver of the giant work vehicle slammed on the brakes, skidding into the small, white Toyota Camry.

The point of no return had passed.

She departed from *this* life . . . and shook the very earth.

In her last weeks, she prayed to be the epicenter of a "Jesus earthquake." She wanted her life to impact people and bring them into a relationship with the God she loves. And it happened, though not as anyone would have expected.

There are certain ways Jeff, Rachel, and I prefer to speak about Kayla's life and passing. We believe words are powerful. One time, while talking to a stranger, I referred to Kayla as "my deceased daughter," and it nearly made Rachel sick. She asked me to never say that again. And I understood why.

Kayla has not ceased to live! Jesus said, "Everyone who lives in me and believes in me will never ever die" (John 11:26 NLT).

In my first post about the accident, I clarified that her beautiful *body* died. Her outer form is no longer in existence, but *she* did not die. Her resurrected soul transitioned to a new home with her Heavenly Father. We are comforted by the reality of her *aliveness* even while we mourn our tremendous loss in this life.

Kayla left an indelible mark on our lives. WE MISS HER SO MUCH! We miss her spunk and confidence, her creativity and intelligence, her uniqueness and sense of humor, her style and personality, her tender heart, and so much more.

Yet we are happy for Kayla. She is in God's loving presence in Paradise—safe, content, and joyful—more alive than ever, move alive than we are! This life is a shadow compared to *that life.*

The Bible says in Isaiah 57:1, "Good people pass away; the godly often die before their time. But no one seems to care or wonder why. No one seems to understand that God is protecting them from the evil to come" (NLT).

As I write in 2020, we are in a lockdown to slow the spread of the dreaded COVID-19 virus. It looks like there could be a colossal impact. The future is uncertain. Fear abounds. Hoarding is rampant. And more terrible events lurk on the horizon. There's a part of me that is thankful Kayla is spared from this.

But you and I are still here. What matters is our character amidst the chaos. We can basically control nothing except our responses, and even that is a challenge! With God's help, we can be people who stand firm—who are wise—who see a bigger picture. We have the chance to put our hope in Him and in His promises. He is our only security. Even if this blows over, the world will face more trials and tragedies. There is no better moment to come close to God. Now is the time.

And you know what? Kayla lived this way even without a worldwide pandemic. Her character reminds me of an evergreen tree with deep roots. Steady, always growing, sheltering her friends as much as she could—yet not without some prickly pine cones of her own. She wasn't perfect, but she knew the One who is perfect, and she trusted Him with every aspect of her life. She flourished in His light.

Conversations with Kelsey

I've had the honor of knowing Kayla since she was a toddler and got to watch her grow up through the years. But I REALLY got to know how wonderful Kayla was (and is) as she and five other girls met with me every Saturday morning. We were going through the book *Crazy Love*. I'm holding Kayla's copy and have tears in my eyes as I'm just now seeing what she underlined from May 2018.

This chapter has a lot about how death is a reality and making an eternal impact with our lives. We talked a lot that particular Saturday about death. I asked, "What regrets would you have if you died today?" Kayla answered: *"I would have no regrets."*

If you are a teen or young adult, you will benefit from seeing where Kayla found her identity and how she understood her place in this world. You will see her concern for the earth and the people and animals who dwell here. You will learn how a quiet girl became a leader, and you will gain understanding from her wisdom. You'll observe how she interacted in her relationships with family, friends, and "enemies" and even how she dealt with romance. I hope this up-close and personal account will help you gain inner strength and an eternal perspective.

Before you continue reading, you can watch this video to see Kayla in action and begin getting to know her.

bit.ly/heartsobig

One-of-a-Kind

"**S**he is like a beloved storybook character," commented a friend when learning more about Kayla's unique interests.

Kayla enjoyed discovering her personality mix as a young preteen. When she read *The Treasure Tree: Helping Kids Understand Their Personality*, she learned that she was like a loyal and kind "golden retriever" but also an organized, industrious, methodical "beaver."

In fifth grade, she likened herself to the ocean.

> If you think about the ocean
> and the beach, but you want
> to know which one is more like
> me, it's the ocean. First of
> all I can get very mad like
> a storm on the sea. I
> can also be very calm like
> the ocean on a nice summer
> day. I have many colorful
> and happy things in me,
> like the bright coral or the
> fun clownfish. I also have
> one ruler who is God and the
> moon represents God.

When Kayla was ten, she went to a writing camp at Miami University in Oxford, Ohio.[2] She wrote this list of things she loved while at the camp. This is the only instance in all of her writings where she mentions a guardian angel.

Things I love:

❖ God
❖ My guardian angel
❖ My family
❖ School
❖ Nature
❖ Peace
❖ The smell of leather
❖ Horses
❖ Nutrition
❖ Dance
❖ Music
❖ Learning
❖ Friends
❖ Water (pool, lake, pond)

Things I don't like:

❖ The devil
❖ The devil's demons
❖ High prices
❖ The mall
❖ Sin
❖ War
❖ Bad Attitudes
❖ The smell of wet hay

---

[2] Six years later, the accident occurred on the way home from that same location. A first responder reported a beautiful woman in a floral dress was at the scene of the accident praying when they arrived. He said there was no car parked on the side of the road and no houses around for her to come from. Afterward he walked up to the tall, youthful woman with long brown hair. He thanked her and told her he wished there were more people like her. Then he turned to walk away. When he looked back, she was gone.

Those who knew Kayla best had the pleasure of seeing her burst forth in hilarity. She definitely had a silly side.

On Christmas day, when she was eleven, the Calabrese family came over to celebrate. It was the most laughter we ever experienced with others. We played a rambunctious acting game in which Kayla had a blast dramatizing bizarre scenarios. We also played *Bean Boozled*. When her turn came to eat a nasty dirty-sock-flavored jelly bean, she chewed and swallowed courageously. Then when others had to eat a gross one, she'd say, "Come on! Just do it!" She convinced me to eat the booger one. I am *still* recovering. Like her dad, she was always up for a disgusting dare. One time, to everyone's shock, Kayla ate a can of spinach for a crazy children's ministry game.

Those preteen years were the cutest years. She developed a "Kayla language" in an adorable tone of voice. When she was tired, she would say, "I tyberd." When she felt cold, she would say, "I colby cheese" and when she was warm and cozy she would say, "I warmy apple." To get my attention, she would quietly say "Mow" in a meowing sort of way instead of "Mom" and she ended many sentences with the nonsensical word "moof."

Kayla had a humorous way of thinking. Some called her witty. Here are a few sentences from a camping trip when she was fifteen.

> *Once we got settled,*
> *we drove to Cucumber Falls,*
> *speculating what type of cucumbers*
> *would be falling. Alas, there was*
> *not a single falling cucumber in*
> *sight.*

At the end of every vacation, she collected dirt from the place where we stayed. She wanted to bring every special location home with her. Another interesting collection was her round glass vase full of metal objects—the rustier the better. Her friends dubbed it her "bowl full of tetanus."

Kayla saw beauty where most saw junk. Her grandma helped me understand that worn and weathered items have particular value because of what they have been through. They possess an untold story. Kayla desired to take decrepit things and make them pulchritudinous (an ugly-sounding word that means beautiful). So she used them to create art.

Every aspect of life held a special place in her heart. At the beginning of each month, she kept track of her favorite new things by drawing little sketches of them. Also, in scrapbook style, she glued ticket stubs, items from simple moments (like finding a feather), and receipts from experiences. She kept track of each detail of the summer along with her thoughts about our family vacations and her time at a youth conference. She also used an app to record a tiny moment of each day her last summer.

Kayla rarely did things the conventional American way. On her phone, she used the Spanish keyboard and military time. When she wrote dates, she put them in day/month/year order. So when I see 10/3/18 in her journal (after she passed), my heart skips a beat until I realize it is March not October. She also used the British version of words (colour, theatre, sabre, etc.) even when her teachers protested.

Another way she bucked against cultural norms was by having a fashion style all her own. In her teen years, her signature look included:

- Hair: any number of braids or a fabric headband.
- Clothing: a long cardigan, flowy blouse, or kimono with a t-shirt that displayed a message (I Have Decided/No Turning Back, Less is More, etc.), jeans or leggings with jean shorts on top.
- Accessories: a key, a compass, or a wrench necklace and sometimes an earthy scarf she knitted. She always wore bracelets—either from events she attended or ones she made.

- Shoes: real-leather combat boots and vintage-style socks.

- Backpack: canvas with heavy duty clips from a military supply store.
- Lunchbag: brown canvas material with a leather strap (sewn by her and her grandma).

She was attractive yet modest. Feminine yet fierce. She was a warrior in God's Kingdom. To her, clothing was a way of making a statement. After she passed, many of her friends wore key necklaces every day with her name engraved on them.

Oh, and guess what her all-time favorite color was? When she was around four years old, if anyone asked, she would launch into her litany: "pink and purple, black and white and gray." We all had the list memorized in that order. But around third grade, she settled on brown. "Chocolate brown" to be exact.

Because of this, the color guard spun beautiful brown flags in Kayla's honor at her memorial. A few weeks later, the student body held a "brown out" night at a football game where they all wore brown and the football players placed a brown KD sticker on their helmets. They dedicated that game to her with a huge banner that read, "One team. One town. One dream. This One's for Kayla."

At youth group, Kayla routinely requested they do a fun dance called "The Interlude." I think she liked it because the tutorial has everyone doing the same motions, but she could improvise and be as expressive as she wanted to be. To celebrate Kayla's sense of fun, many of her friends went on the stage during her memorial service and danced to the Interlude. Later, when some of her closest friends graduated, they celebrated by dancing to it again.

Once during a Superbowl party, Kayla began braiding her friend Kendall's long brown hair in micro braids. She recruited more friends to join. By the end of the game, her entire head was covered. Kendall went to school the next day looking wild. During Kayla's last winter break, she put her own hair in numerous tiny braids.

During spirit week at her high school, students wore themed clothes each day. Kayla participated but in subtle ways such as wearing bracelets that matched the color of the day and two different colors of combat boots on "crazy day."

Kayla and a friend came up with the idea to fold a lot of paper cranes and place

them all over their drama club set probably just to make people wonder. In the few days between Kayla's accident and her memorial service, her friends folded 1,000 paper cranes in her honor. Jeff joined others just two weeks later in passing them out on the first day back to school. They also filled a huge jar of them and wrote memories on the papers before folding them. Jeff, Rachel, and I cherished opening a few every night for a long time.

At lunchtimes, Kayla always wanted to read, but her best friend Ashley would keep talking to her until she'd laugh or choke. Kayla acted like she wasn't paying attention, but she couldn't resist her friend's rousing stories.

On days when Kayla brought celery to lunch, she'd peel off the strings because she didn't like the texture and place them at Ashley's spot. Other times, Kayla ate a whole peeled cucumber, one of her all-time favorite foods. Her youth pastor, John Calabrese, always bought one for her when he was buying food for the students. Her typical after-school snack was something cold like frozen mango or paletas (popsicles). And she was often crunching on plain ice. But she also craved warm carbs and had an affection for tea time in the winter. She refused to eat apples and bananas because they made her stomach feel "weird."

There were two special desserts she made from scratch by herself. One was marshmallows. The other was French macarons. I was surprised when she decided to make something so fancy the evening before a week long youth group trip. The process took five hours, but she enjoyed it and didn't stress out (like I would have).

Kayla loved the rain! As a child she would stand at the door to watch thunderstorms and the "dancing trees" (as she called them) with her grandma at their house. Kayla declared herself a "pluviophile" (someone who finds joy and peace of mind during rainy days). She even wrote a prayer asking God to help her not be sad on sunny days! Whenever possible, as soon as drops would start coming down, she would run around outside barefoot.

I remember an unusually warm November night when Kayla was twelve. Our church was celebrating a Thanksgiving meal together when a torrential downpour started. She and a few friends and leaders all purposefully got soaked, and they had a romping good time!

Whenever it rained during youth group, all the students knew she would splash in the puddles afterward, and many joined her. After she passed, the whole group danced in the rain in her honor.

On a warm summer evening, Kayla and her grandma had just completed sewing her floral kimono, and she was feeling satisfied. Her happiness increased because clouds were rolling in. Grandma got Kayla's attention as she was sitting on their sidewalk waiting for us to pick her up and quickly snapped the iconic pic of Kayla looking back over her shoulder. As rain started to fall, Kayla sprawled out on the sidewalk so that when she arose, the wet cement made an outline of her body.

She was a tree climber. We have many pictures of these moments as she grew up, but the last tree she climbed was when Ashley parked under a low-lying branch. Kayla climbed onto it through the sunroof.

Kayla also loved fire! The mysterious ways the flames moved captured her attention. Whenever she went camping, she and her grandma wanted to stay and watch the embers until they were completely consumed. The last get-together with her friends at our house involved a huge bonfire to celebrate surviving pre-band camp.

As quirky as she was, Kayla was also steady, consistent, and dependable. Every Sunday morning, she sat in the far left seat of the front row of the auditorium. Then, every Sunday night at youth group, she sat in the far right seat of the front row in the same auditorium. Everyone knew where to find her.

When she had a role, she didn't want anyone else to fill it. She cherished being the hair-stylist for her friends. One time Kaelie allowed someone else to braid her hair exactly like Kayla would do it. When Kayla saw her, she gave her that "I'm not pleased with you" look. Kayla also became angry with her sister when Rachel did one of her chores. She called it "one of the most annoying things EVER." Here is one of Kayla's chore charts she made.

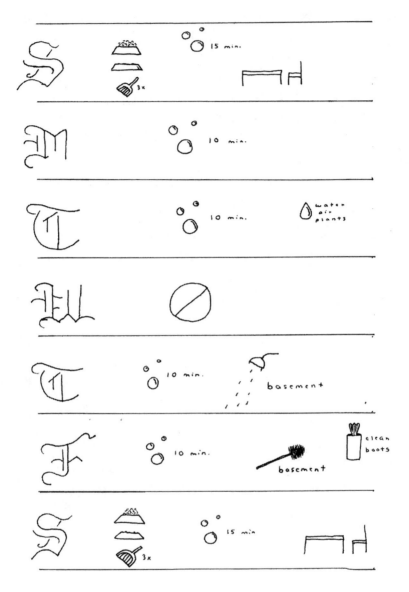

As a minimalist, Kayla was known for her cleaning and organizational skills and used them to help her friends declutter their rooms (which they appreciated). Likewise, she helped manage items in our home. She kept her closet with perfectly spaced clothing on hangers arranged by color and also folded neatly in her drawers. Her methodical and patient ways helped me whenever I needed a knot in a necklace undone. She enjoyed restoring order to the world.

When she was fourteen, she explained in her journal, "If I think I'm being pressured to do something I don't want to do, I fight back even harder." Then she added, "Also, my friends have fun taking pictures of me and watching my reaction." Kayla was not a "selfie" girl. She proved it by often collapsing to the ground whenever someone tried to take a picture of her.

Kayla made these statements about herself four days before she departed.

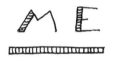

does not like

stupidity, redundancy, small talk, emotional outbursts, illogical arguments, incompetence, disorganisation, manipulation

I

N

T

J

introvert

intuitive

thinker

judger

i'm an ancient soul, in a modern body, with a futuristic state of mind.

aesthetic

red hot embers, newspapers, minimalism, the sound of pouring rain, chess, antithetical statements, blizzards, secret passages, ciphers, petrichor, carrying books to class, paint covered hands, mystery books before bed, matte black, staring at the stars, lists, hot tea in the morning, death stares

SLYTHERIN

ambition
* i set goals & i reach them

Someone described her personality as "hard shell–hot lava." At times, she was perceived as intimidating, but she was full of the flowing love of Jesus. Even people who didn't know Kayla personally could sense that love. A thoughtful student recently texted:

> *"She always had such a beautiful spirit and although she was quiet, she carried herself with a sort of lightness and happiness that I always admired. Know that Kayla brought light into many people's lives, even those she didn't know."*

∞∞∞∞∞

It amazes me how God created such variety in personalities. He loves our uniqueness. The second greatest commandment in the Bible is "Love others *as you love yourself.*"[3] If you don't know your personality type, discovering and celebrating it will help you value yourself (and others) the way God intended. Kayla would encourage you: get to know who God made you to be.

[3] Paraphrase of Mark 12:31.

There's No Place Like Home

I ♡ MY TOWN

In 2001, Jeff and I lived thirty minutes outside of New York City. On 9/11 we sat stunned, watching the smoke rising from the rubble of the Twin Towers from the hillside behind my office. It was unbelievable. You would think a national tragedy would make us *not want* to bring a child into this world, but God had other plans. About a week later, after four years of marriage, we both suddenly had an irresistible desire to have a baby!

Kayla was born in New Jersey, which she always claimed with pride, even though we moved to Ohio three weeks later. Jeff was beginning his doctoral studies in Cincinnati. Our starter home was a 1923 saltbox colonial that Jeff renovated in a sketchy neighborhood. I'll never forget when a pit bull rushed down our driveway at Kayla and me. In the nick of time, I shut the chain link gate, scooped her up, and ran into the house. It was a close call.

Her little sister arrived on the scene when Kayla was twenty-one months old, and we were so glad she surprised us. Rachel completed our little family.

I was a homemaker while Jeff studied and started a business flipping homes and later renting them. He worked long, hard hours to provide for us, but when he was home, he poured his energy into those little girls. Together we saturated them with love, prayers, and fun.

We moved to our second house after a few years. It was on a quiet cul-de-sac near many conveniences, including a library at the end of our street (lucky for young Kayla). It was hard for me to leave less than two years later. I reluctantly said goodbye, not only to the location but to friends I loved. It was time to move to a small-yet-growing city to help start a church. Not long after, I became thankful that God led us to Harrison.

This is where Kayla spent the rest of her years. We made our home in a cedar chalet. When she first stepped into this house as a six-year-old, she looked it over and declared, "I love all the woodwork!"

Spending most of her time in this setting was perfect for her interests. She revelled in the solitude, being surrounded by wildlife and our neighbors' farm animals. She spent oodles of hours reading without interruption.

She preferred being home over anywhere except for the times she attended God-centered conferences that gave her a taste of heaven.

Conversations with Kelsey

We were at Bob Evans one of the last times I ever talked to Kayla. She had just returned from her trip to New York and was telling me all about it.

KELSEY: Girls, where would you love to live one day? What would your dream house look like?

Most of the girls and I started throwing out all sorts of ideas. From Victorian houses to treehouses to farmhouses . . . we started dreaming, but I noticed Kayla was quiet and wasn't contributing. I knew how creative Kayla is and wondered why she wasn't expressing all of her creative dreams.

KELSEY: Kayla, what does your dream house look like?

When I think back on what she said, I get goosebumps.

KAYLA: My house *is* my dream house.

KELSEY: I mean when you grow up. What do you imagine your future house looking like?

KAYLA: I don't know. I can't really picture myself living in any other house than the one I live in right now. It's perfect.

So when you read about her life, imagine her in a midwestern town with a mix of suburban neighborhoods, agricultural areas, small shopping plazas, and a quaint old downtown. The churches in our city are phenomenal, and their partnership with the schools is unprecedented. It's a special community, yet has its share of problems. She attended schools in old buildings that had excellent teachers. Most could challenge Kayla's insatiable desire for knowledge. And thankfully, new school buildings are under construction.

kaylaskyemarie1010

Friday night football games were the big events. There is a classic, long-standing, next-town-over rivalry that got out of hand between the two marching bands. They were not allowed to play at the same events *for years* because of violence that erupted between them a decade before. It was Kayla's desire for connection that brought them together in solidarity after she passed. You can see what happened here:

bit.ly/ConnectionECHarrison

Overall, Kayla loved our city and made the best of her circumstances. Yet she never totally felt like she belonged. She was a temporary resident. And truly, aren't we all?

> All these people were still living by faith when they died. They did not receive the things promised; they only saw them and welcomed them from a distance, admitting that they were foreigners and strangers on earth . . . Therefore God is not ashamed to be called their God, for he has prepared a city for them. Hebrews 11:13,16 NIV

Kayla wrote this from a devotional when she was fourteen.

> Your New Location
>
> Bible Reading: Philippians 1:21
>
> "For to me, living means living for Christ, and dying is even better."
>
> Truth: For a Christian, death just means moving to a better place.
>
> Dare: Get ready for your new home.

What's in a Name

Kayla Marie Duerler
(Pronounced "Der-ler"—darn that extra vowel!)

When Jeff and I arrived at Toccoa Falls College to start our sophomore year, we met to share our summer experiences since we were newly dating. He told me the story of a precious girl that melted his heart on a mission trip to Mexico. It's the only thing I remember from the conversation.

A little girl named Keila in a kids' program was drawn to Jeff even though he wasn't accustomed to caring for children. Something about their brief connection left an abiding impact. He encountered something new—the love of a child. From the moment he told me about her, I filed away the idea: if we get married and if we ever have a daughter, her name will be K-a-y-l-a. I immediately chose that spelling because of my middle name which means "rejoice."

Sometimes the meaning of names is prophetic. If that were ever true, I think it's the case with Kayla whose name means "wise child" and "pure."

I wrote this prayer before she was born, "I want a child like Samuel. One who is set apart for You, obedient, listening, hearing Your voice and speaking with *wisdom* in a way that helps others and reaches far and wide."

Kayla knew her name meant "wise child," and she owned it. She prayed often for God to give her wisdom, and He answered those prayers as He promised in the Bible:

> If any of you lacks wisdom, you should ask God, who gives generously to all without finding fault, and it will be given to you. James 1:5 NIV

When she was seven, I recorded this interaction in her memory book:

> Kayla, you told me about two books you read that I wouldn't be happy about. After a splendid night of family fun, I laid in your bed, and we were chatting and praying. I explained that "Kayla" not only means "wise child" but also "pure." This led to a discussion about protecting our hearts and choosing carefully what we watch and read. You decided that from now on, when you're reading a story and your stomach gets those "butterflies," you'll stop and find another book to read. I also reminded you to confess to God when you allow something to make your heart or mind impure, and He will cleanse you, but you might not forget what you saw or read, and that is why we have to protect ourselves. I also shared the beautiful verse, "Above all else, guard your heart for it is the wellspring of life."[4] You accepted everything we talked about. You are a wise child!

I was always protective of the girls about what we viewed. When I was young, I saw scenes of movies that I couldn't unsee when I was spending time at friends' houses. My mind was scarred, and I didn't want my girls to experience that. So I made it a practice to

---

[4] Paraphrase of Proverbs 4:23.

change the channel or turn off shows and even commercials that went against God's heart or holy character. Some might say I was overprotective, but I have no regrets about this.

> I will not set before my eyes anything that is worthless.
> Psalm 101:3 ESV

In seventh grade, Kayla chose purity as her theme of the year, and we witnessed her living it out. She was careful with her book and media choices. We see evidence of her passion for purity in the end of a letter she wrote to herself that year. It was intended to be given back to her upon graduation. Her postscript admonishes herself to stay pure.

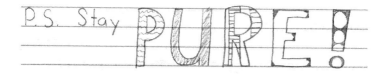

We made sure she understood that her purity comes from God. Jesus was the only human who lived a 100% pure life, and as a perfect sacrifice, He took the punishment we deserved. When we accept him, we are exchanging our impurity for His purity. She recognized that she could never be perfectly righteous and that she needed His righteousness. It is on that basis that she lives in Heaven with the Holy One.

Unfortunately, she didn't escape this earth without some scars. My heart sank when I learned that she overheard many dirty conversations between boys on the bus ride home in eighth grade. She was uncomfortable but never told me until later. She didn't want to inconvenience me, but I would have gladly driven her every day to protect her heart and mind.

Why did we give her the middle name Marie? I considered the name Skye solely because I liked the way it sounded. But the name Marie held significance. We have close friends and family with this name. These ladies and our relationships with them trumped a "cool" name!

Jeff was drawn to Marie because it is a form of Mary. He prayed for Kayla as an infant that she would be humble and receptive to God's will. I wrote in Kayla's memory book when she was four: "Kayla, you are enthralled with the true story of Christmas. Every day you play as if you are Mary. We love how your demeanor is one of serenity." Kayla's posture before the Lord was more than just pretend play.

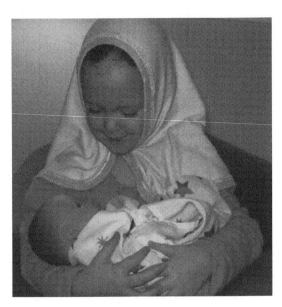

On a humorous note, I added to the entry: "We visited a live nativity scene, and you were visibly disappointed because the lady portraying Mary looked like she was eighty-years-old! I had to whisper and explain that she wasn't the real Mary. You were relieved."

Kayla valued our middle name choice, though as a teen she also wished to be called Skye. Kayla loved the uniqueness of it. Plus, she and Rachel both love the actual sky, always mesmerized by the formations of clouds, the shades of blue in the daytime, other hues at sunrise and sunset, and the stars at night. My girls are the ones who taught me to look up and admire the atmosphere above not just the plants and trees on the ground below.

Around the age of fourteen, Kayla incorporated Skye while still honoring Marie by creating her online name for three social media platforms. She called herself Skye Marie on Society6 and YouTube (her profile picture is her pink flower) and her Instagram account was @kaylaskyemarie1010.

∞∞∞∞

We are so pleased that Kayla lived up to her name. We believe it was not a random chance that we named her Kayla Marie. God guided and directed us. He knows all things.

Isaiah 49:1

Listen to me, you islands; hear this, you distant nations: Before I was born, the Lord called me; from my mother's womb he has spoken my name.

God created us with a plan in mind. He cares about us and wants to see us fulfill his plan.

Have you considered that God knew *you* before you were born? You are special and loved just as Kayla is. I pray that you fulfill the destiny God has for your life no matter what your name means.

Kindness and Generosity

As Kayla was growing up, I recorded many ways she revealed a servant's heart. Sometimes I witnessed her actions first hand, and other times they would come out through conversations at the dinner table or before bed. No matter how small, each act that I chronicled was special, but when I pieced them together, I was struck by the overall impact.

Even as a toddler, Kayla helped me every way she could. When I was in the last stages of pregnancy with Rachel, Kayla picked things up for me. She assisted me in prepping meals as much as she was able. We have a cute video of her washing potatoes with a scrub brush. Then, when Rachel was born, she helped with bath time. She squirted her head with water, threw away her diaper, opened her fresh diaper, combed her hair, and put her dirty clothes down the laundry chute.

In March of second grade, I wrote to her:

> As I was shampooing your hair the other night, I asked you to tell me three things about your day. You told me you and your friends were filling in the four-square grid with sidewalk chalk. On a side note, you mentioned that you used all the little nubs of chalk because your friends were afraid that they would scrape their fingers on the ground. You weren't looking for praise, but I was so proud of you and shared what Jesus says about true love in friendship. It's laying down your life and serving others. I said, "If Jesus were there, He would have done the same thing you did." Kayla, you have the gift of serving, and it is beautiful my dear one!

In third grade, many of the kids in Kayla's class were being unkind to one of their classmates. They treated him like he was gross, and if he touched them, they would say, "ewww" and then wipe that spot onto someone else. Kayla refused to be a part of this. When they wiped it onto her, she did not wipe it off. She had compassion for the mistreated boy and refused to join the mockery.

That same school year, her teacher gave the writing prompt: "You just won $1000!" She responded:

by: Kayla

I just won $1,000 in a split-the-pot drawing! I'm going to give a quarter of it to a charity for the poor and homeless another quarter of it I'm going to use to buy bibles for soldiers. The 3rd quarter I will use by giving it to disaster realif fund and the last quarter I'll put in tithe to help my church grow so more people can learn about Jesus.

On the bus rides home, Kayla chose to sit with Kennedy, one of her closest friends, every *other* day so she could sit with her little sister as well. It would have been natural for Kayla to sit with her friend, but she didn't want Rachel to be alone.

During a field trip that I helped chaperone, one of the moms could not ride on the bus, so Kayla invited her daughter to squeeze into our seat. Despite the uncomfortable, hot, and humid conditions, we had a special time together playing travel games. The girl's mom wrote a little message to Kayla after she passed, "You gave my daughter the gift of comfort during a field trip. And now you have given her the gift of comfort by helping to lead her to the Lord by your faith. Thank you, beautiful girl."

I wrote to her in July of 2012, "We celebrated your tenth birthday with Kennedy and Morgan by serving at Matthew 25 Ministries. It was your plan for over half a year. I love your heart to help others!" A year before, Kayla reached out to Morgan because she was new to our church and didn't have friends there yet.

As a twelve-year-old, she prayed:

Master,

    Thank you for the kindness you've bestowed upon me. Please help me be kind and gentle to other people.

When she was fifteen, she spent a day serving at a pregnancy center. Later that summer, she spent time with our church family repainting playground equipment at a local elementary school. Then she dedicated one morning during Christmas break to painting positive quotes on the bathroom walls of her former elementary school with the art club. After she passed, Mrs. Cummings, one of Kayla's favorite art teachers, led groups to paint quotes from Kayla's journals on the walls of the high school during a "Day of Service." The cheer-leaders helped me paint this one.

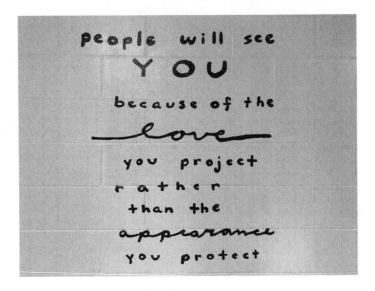
people will see
YOU
because of the
love
you project
rather
than the
appearance
you protect

The other is "Things are going to get hard. Be strong. Persist." It ended up being such a timely statement with the pandemic just eighteen months away!

One cold day, she traveled with her youth group to downtown Cincinnati to talk and pray with the homeless. Kayla's youth group made it a point to treat the people they met with dignity. She told me that she was struck by their need for people to acknowledge their names and their existence.

Kayla often gave her time and talents to show personalized love. For friends and family, she spent countless hours knitting Christmas gifts one winter break. She also made watercolor paintings, cards, and embroidery thread bracelets for loved ones. And anyone who gave a gift to Kayla received a personalized thank you note in return.

The high school library had a cart of free books. Kayla regularly checked it, and whenever a Shakespeare showed up, she took it home. When she had about ten, she stacked and tied them together with a ribbon as a gift. The next day Kayla brought them to the lunch table and waited for her friend, who was a fan of Shakespeare, to arrive. Gabby appreciated Kayla's thoughtfulness.

Kindness was not always natural for Kayla. It was a discipline she worked on. She knew she needed God's help.

If I let Jesus have control,
I'd be a lot kinder.

BE KIND!

listen
don't correct her word choice
don't shut her down mid-sentence
don't snap at her as if the answer
    was obvious
compliment her w/o a prompt
give her gifts
show-don't-tell

Before Kayla entered high school, she wrote this letter:

Dear Future Self, I want to remind you of a few things. First, you are not super mature now that you are in high school. Don't look down on people . . . You're equals. Another thing, do something nice for Mama and Padre. Take time to clean the table or do the dishes. Lastly, people look up to you. When back in school, be kind. Walk the Jesus walk. Give someone

your pencil if they ask (with a smile) and
be less sarcastic.

Our family sponsors two girls in Kenya who are the same ages as Kayla and Rachel. She wrote letters, drew them pictures, and prayed for them. She noted that she wanted her friends to sponsor a child for her birthday when she was turning fifteen.

Kayla was a giver. When she and I were on our way home from church one afternoon, we discussed her new giving commitment. She wanted to give a huge percentage of her money to help build a high school in Kenya and our new church facility here. I replied that giving so much was noble but not sustainable in the grownup world. This was three months before Kayla went to be with the Lord.

When I saw her commitment card, it was even more generous than she told me. I see in her notes where she wrote different amounts until she landed on committing 60% of her money for the next two years on top of her ongoing 20% tithe. Her perspective toward money was proof of her values. She wanted to reach the world with God's love through her church.

She kept this card in her wallet as a reminder of where her money belonged.

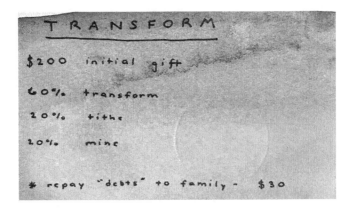

TRANSFORM

$200 initial gift

60% transform

20% tithe

20% mine

* repay "debts" to family - $30

After Kayla passed, we heard testimonies of her kindness. Two girls came up to me the night of the accident when we were gathered at LifeSpring. They said, with tears in their eyes, "We are here because Kayla told us we are special and beautiful." Just days later, a student from the high school sent us a Facebook message: "Kayla and I only had one class together, and she always talked to me when nobody else did because I didn't have a lot of friends." Another teenage girl told me how when she was feeling depressed, Kayla sat with her and told her she is beautiful and that God loves her. Another student said: "Every day in the hall last year she told me to smile and that I was worth it."

Her friend Kaelie from color guard wrote:

> I remember the first time I came to youth group was because she invited me to a movie night. We were at guard, and she had asked me about my faith. I could always go to her with my questions and she always helped me, even if she didn't know the answer right away. It's amazing to me how much perseverance she had in leading others to be a disciple!

Within days after Kayla went to be with Jesus, a student named Lyndsi made a decision. She was in the high school business program and had the idea to start a subscription box company but had not yet figured out what to put in the boxes. After being inspired by Kayla's journal entries and prayers, she named her company Cultivate Kindness.[5] Lyndsi packs the boxes with items that give people practical ways to show kindness and make a difference.

When Kayla was thirteen, she wrote a list of qualities she would like people to remember if she were gone:

---

[5] cultivatekindnessbox.com

① Write a list of qualities you would like people to remember about you if you were gone. Ask God to help of you be someone who is "always doing something good."

II) Look for good qualities in you friends and family members. Tell them today how much you appreciate them for those things.

① joyful
patient
lovIng
KInd
cReAtIvE
[Smart]
un poco crazy

② ☺ K

Dear Lord,
THANK YOU FOR EVERYTHING.
THANK YOU FOR EVERYTHING.
I'm sorry for almost being grumpy. PLEASE help ME to BE remembered FOR doing GOOD things.
In Jesus' Name,
Amen

Kayla, your prayer is answered. We remember the good things you've done.

∞∞∞∞∞∞

Let's actively show kindness and generosity to others. To a hurting world, we may never know how big an impact our simple loving actions can make.

Bibliophile

bib·li·o·phile /ˈbiblēəˌfīl/ n. A lover of books;
Someone who finds joy and peace of mind
while holding a quality book

Kayla's attraction to books started early. Before she could read on her own, we read to her daily. At first we used the same books over and over again because they were all we had. She ate them up—literally! I found her in her crib one day after a nap with the spine of a book in her mouth. She chewed little bites all down the edge. Hence, books in her crib became a no-no.

At twenty months, she followed our example and pretended to read books to her baby doll. As she grew, her interests expanded to hundreds of picture books. Thank God for the library, or we'd be broke. Humorous ones were her preference. *Little Pea* (the pea's parents wanted it to eat candy), *Little Hoot* (the owl that didn't want to stay up at night), and *Little Oink* (the pig that wanted to keep its room clean) made her laugh every time. The reverse psychology and ironic humor struck a chord with her.

Once she began reading on her own, chapter books began filling our home, then adolescent literature, and even the classics. We listened to audiobooks in the car and as we worked in the kitchen together. I remember listening to the Laura Ingalls Wilder series the summer before fourth grade. We shivered to *The Long Winter* while the actual weather was blazing.

In elementary school, she and Kennedy were always the top two readers, and they were the only students who ever out-read Mrs. Haas, their TAG (Talented and Gifted) teacher from fourth through eighth grade.

Over the span of her life, we checked out thousands of books from the library. Kayla went online to reserve as many as she wanted so she had a constant supply. When we brought them home, she stacked skyscrapers of borrowed books around our bookshelves because they couldn't all fit otherwise. Although fines accrued when we occasionally didn't renew them in time, I figured the library deserved the money for all the extra work Kayla caused. If she just used her Kindle, there would be no fines, but she always preferred paper to e-books. I can only imagine how upset Kayla would have been during the pandemic with the libraries being closed for so many months.

Amid her constantly reading four or five books at a time, I thought, "There's no way for her to keep track of what's going on in each story without getting them jumbled!" But I was wrong. She refused my advice to simplify. That noggin of hers kept track of every setting, plot, and character.

One of the two letters to her future graduating self was entirely about books. She included lists of resources that she recommended to her older self, including non-fiction, adult-level books such as *Winning with People* and *Say Goodbye to Survival Mode*. Kayla read a wide range of books, not just fantasy. Life skills were important to her.

Our pets loved her steady presence. She was never alone as she traveled into stories. Her sweet little companions took turns sitting with her.

Though Kayla looked calm while reading, she was focused and speedy. Pages turned like clockwork. Occasionally, but not often, she would let out a little cry of disbelief or excitement depending on the events in the story.

Her frequent entrance into the written world gave Kayla and her friends Gabby, Alex, and Emma a winning idea in 2016. Mrs. Haas gave groups of her students the opportunity to enter the National Spelling Bee's Spellebrity video contest. Kayla was only thirteen when she filmed and edited "Fairytale Escape."

bit.ly/SpellingBeeEscapeArtists

The three-and-a-half minute video features three young people being united in friendship by the stories they are reading. To help communicate the story and meet the guidelines, Kayla silently interspersed three spelling words and definitions one at a time between action scenes. It was such a compelling work that the judges selected them as one of the top entrants in the nation.

We nearly missed the opportunity to take part, though. When I received a voicemail, I heard the first part and ignored the rest. I thought it was spam, like a bogus "You've won a Sweepstakes" message, so I disregarded it. Kayla described the situation in third person as telling a story:

After the video was sent in, life went back to normal, that is, until one afternoon the Escape Artists found out that one of the other teams from Mrs. Haas' class made it past the first cut. The team went home feeling rejected. The next day after school, Kayla found out that her team had made it past the first cut and the judges needed a form in one hour! Stressed, she frantically tried everything she could but it was too late. The deadline passed. The four girls were helpless until Kayla's mom got an extension for them. The judges received the papers on time.

The top ten videos were to be announced in a few days and The Escape Artists were excited. The night before the scheduled announcement, Kayla had the urge to check the website. To her astonishment, the top ten videos were already posted and Fairytale Escape was there!

Master,

    Thank you for the amazing opportunity of Spellebrity! If you want me to go to D.C., please give us votes. We put our votes in your hands.

The next step was to rally enough online votes to get into the top five teams, each member of which would be flown with a parent to Washington D.C. So our friends, family, and even kind people we didn't know supported the team. We were so excited when we heard the great news. They were in third place.

Stellar spellers headed to D.C.

Harry Kane
Harrison Press Staff

Four students from Harrison Junior School are semifinalists in a national video spelling competition, and are heading to Washington D.C. at the end of the month on an all expenses paid trip for an awards banquet to see if they will win the contest outright.

All across the nation, kids partake in spelling bee competitions, but this year something new was added to the mix.

In the debut year of the video contest, students produced, directed and edited their own short videos that included three words that would be useful to know in a spelling bee.

Students brainstormed and created videos of up to five minutes in length that captures the idea.

"This is the first year that they've done this video contest," said Bev Haas, English language arts teacher at Harrison's Junior School.

The Harrison Junior School eighth-grade students placed third in the national competition, and will showcase their video, and be judged at the awards banquet from May 22-27.

The five finalists get a "clean slate" going into the final round, explained Haas.

During Bee Week, the five teams will present their videos to the 285 national spelling bee finalists, who will vote to crown the champion team.

The members of the champion team will each receive $1,000 and a trophy.

Kayla Duerler, Gabby Brander, Alexandra Miller and Emma Chamblin were the finalists who formed the group called, "The Escape Artists," and created the video as part of their English language arts eighth-grade class project at the Junior School.

The four students worked on the project for three weeks, and then completed the video assignment over spring break.

Two other students were recruited as actors in the video. Their names are Christian Mauldin and Lydia Harrison.

Kayla Duerler was the camera operator and the editor of the video project. She used her Canon camera and editing software.

The name of their video is called, *Fairy Tale Escape.*

Four students from Harrison Junior School are semifinalists in a national video spelling competition, and are heading to Washington D.C. at the end of the month on an all expenses paid trip for an awards banquet. From left: Emma Chamblin, Kayla Duerler, Alexandra Miller and Gabby Brander.

The video is about three situations that kids go through," said Gabby Brander, spokesperson for the eighth-grade team.

Brander said that the video portrays issues that kids go through.

"They go to a book of fairy tales and that serves as their escape to take them out of the bad world and put them into the story," said Bradner.

The three words used in the video are asylum, pulchritude and vituperative.

"One of them was a girl being bullied, one of them a boy's parents was fighting and one of them a girl was homeless and was in a bad situation," said Bradner.

The group worked on a few different ideas before coming up with the fairy tale concept.

"We came up, originally, with a few different ideas and then we decided which direction we wanted to go in, because one was a fun idea and this is a more of a serious topic," she said.

Judges evaluated the videos on criteria such as inspirational quality, relevance, creativity, and the inclusion of three words, which would be great to know for a spelling bee.

The E.W. Scripps Company puts on the competition, and it was presented by Kindle.

Students receive a Kindle Paperwhite e-reader, hotel, air travel, and are given a tour of Washington D.C., tickets to the zoo, and a $400 gift card to defray costs.

The Spellebrity video contest team finalists were Mary N. from Oneonta, NY; Lexi's Productions from New Haven, Ind.; The Escape Artists from Harrison,; Just read It from Lake Oswego, Ore., and Nathan & Nice from Cincinnati, Ohio.

Visit spellebrity.com or the Bee's YouTube channel to view the five Finalis videos! Which team do you think will win it all?

Copyright
Register Publications, 2016
91st Year, No. 16

That adventure became one of our best mother/daughter experiences. While there, we explored museums, the National Zoo, and the White House.

The Scripps National Spelling Bee treated the girls like celebrities. They sat on the big, bright stage after their video played for a Q & A session in front of hundreds of spellers. We attended the spelling bee finals and the banquet. Though our team didn't win, the girls were blessed beyond expectation. It was especially great for Kayla because six months earlier she chose to *not* go on the eighth grade D.C. trip. As an introvert, she didn't want to be exhausted from being around rambunctious classmates nonstop, so this trip was perfect for her.

I was blessed because Kayla enjoyed being with me even after I broke my toe on the base of the hotel bed on the second-to-last day of the trip. We were stuck in the room with my foot elevated, but Kayla and I were content to watch TV and to eat room service meals together—just the two of us.

While there, she ran out of her own books. I recall her reading the book I brought along, *Inside the Teenage Brain*. I never finished a full chapter before *she* finished the whole thing. At that point, Kayla officially knew more about parenting a teen than I did!

On a special note, it was a privilege to baptize Emma, Alex, and her mom Shelly at Kayla's memorial service. Like the message of the Spellebrity video, her teammates in "Fairy Tale Escape" will reunite again in another world where all conflict and distress will be absent.

Starting the next year, Kayla became involved in the book club. The Library Facilitator sent us a letter after Kayla passed.

Mr. and Mrs. Duerler,

I want to express my deepest condolences to you and take a moment to share some of my memories of Kayla.

I got to know Kayla last year when she joined our book club at school. She quickly became our unofficial leader and recruiter. Her enthusiasm for reading was contagious. We have never had a student who kept a journal of the books she read!

It is always cool to hear the students discuss the books at our meetings - to watch how their minds are working. Kayla was confident in articulating her beliefs and values, but her approach to opinions different from her own impressed me the most. It reminded me of 1 Peter 3:15 - doing so with gentleness and respect.

I also got to see Kayla's creative side. At the end of the year, she created a design for each of the books we had read. At our last meeting, we were able to use her designs to make a button for each book. I have included one of our buttons with this letter.

At that time, Kayla also recommended a book for us to read - *A Darker Shade of Magic* by V. E. Schwab. We met recently and decided that would be our first book of the year.

In closing, I want to thank you for sharing Kayla with our public school system. As a Christian mother, I know that is not a decision taken lightly. Sometimes, our kids are exposed to things that we would rather they not see or hear. I am so glad I got the chance to know Kayla, even for a little bit. She was and will continue to be a light shining in our school.

Sincerely,

Pam Hopkins
Library Facilitator
Wm. Henry Harrison High School

Kayla knew that books and even certain shows and movies occupied a lot of her time—and her heart. I see many times where she tells herself to not let books become her idol, or she comes up with strategies to discipline herself from watching too many episodes. She made a note to find an app for self-control because stories occupied most of her spare moments. For example, while in a class, if a teacher started skipping down a rabbit trail, she felt no obligation to pay attention. Her immediate response was to disappear into the fantasy world through a book until the academic lecture resumed.

Kayla always read a book while navigating the high school halls, never running into anyone.

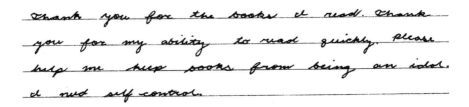

When receiving a new book, she would sometimes exclaim, "Look how gorgeous this is!" while running her hand over the cover in admiration. Then she placed it on her bookshelf by color, creating an aesthetically pleasing library in her room. She added decorative elements like painted door knobs and locks to complete the setting.

Not long ago, I thought I would make a post about these unusual decorations, but I wasn't sure what to say. The very next day, my mentor called and said she was thinking about Kayla's locks and how perfect they are on a bookshelf because doorknobs and books both lead to new places.

Kayla created a separate journal of book reviews. The way she communicates in them is like hearing her speak in person. They are "so Kayla" and such fun to read. In each one, she cites the author and the title which she lettered in the style of the book cover.

Six
OF
CROWS

LEIGH
BARDUGO

I don't even know where to begin
when talking about this book. I loved
almost everything: the characters, the
romances, the magic use, the main
plot, the plot twists, the backstories,
and the writing. My one problem is
that the plot slowed down at moments.
I'm super impressed at the improvement
that Leigh made after the Grisha trilogy.

CROOKED KINGDOM

LEIGH BARDUGO

How is this book even better than six of crows? I'm so impressed! It's really the ending that made it a 5 star book. I almost cried.

HEIDI

johanna spyri

This book was so cute! It's tone was lighthearted and brought me back to my childhood. I remember reading the abridged version at home. Heidi reminds me of Anne in her positivity. What a wholesome book!

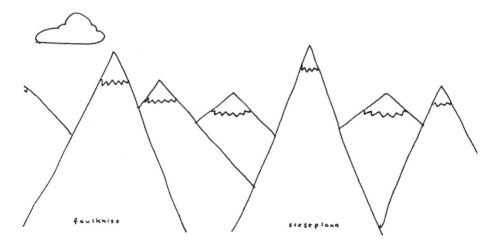

faulkniss   sceseplana

MOONCOP
TOM GAULD

This was a melancholy graphic novel about people leaving the mooncop behind on the moon. It was gorgeous and unsettling & amazing. The drawings are beautiful!

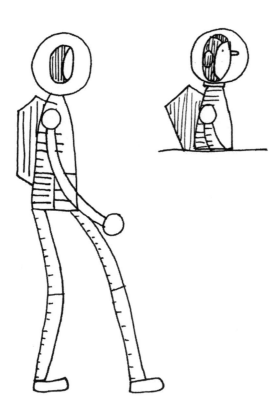

As much as the look of books appealed to her, she didn't judge a book by its cover. It was the *content* that mattered the most. And for older books that weren't so attractive, she'd open them and take in their aroma. For most people, the mustiness is unpleasant. But to Kayla, it spoke of history, knowledge, and adventure—a beauty all its own.

One Saturday in her last October, we took a day trip to a quaint town. Kayla was thrilled to discover an old bookstore. She told us to leave her there, do everything else, then come back to get her. Although we didn't agree to leave her there alone, we did give her some extra time perusing the shelves. The following summer, less than a month before she passed, her Grandma Duerler took her to a vintage bookstore in Cincinnati. Micky enjoyed watching Kayla's delight as she took in all the books. She was amazed at the variety of genres Kayla bought. Going there was a bucket list item, and they had a special time—so much so, that when they did not return when expected on 8-8-18, one thought I had was, "maybe they did a spontaneous field trip to another bookstore."

Before that final day, Kayla spent seven months making BookTube videos for her YouTube channel. She wanted to connect with more bibliophiles. She explains why she braved starting a channel in her first video. She answers the question "Why do you love reading?" with "It's a way to escape from the world." Then as you watch her recordings from the early days to the last ones, you see Kayla grow in freedom to show the full range  of her personality. In them we see her many sides: shy, silly, sarcastic, and even vivacious. She thrived on this platform and revelled in interacting with other voracious readers.

bit.ly/SkyeMarieBookTube

To honor Kayla's love of reading after her passing, one of the local elementary schools collected children's books that were donated in her name. Then a few weeks later, high school teacher Mrs. Johnson had an idea. Seeing how many students had to wait after school for rides, she thought to honor Kayla with lending libraries that would be located near the entrances of three schools. With the help of students, she had them constructed out of old barn wood which Kayla would appreciate.

∞∞∞∞

One day, Jeff asked Kayla where she wanted to live if she could choose anywhere. He thought Spain or somewhere Mediterranean would come out of her mouth, but her answer surprised him. She said, "Rivendell," Tolkein's timeless realm in the immortal elves' hidden valley. It is a place where people of all races find refuge and healing.

Kayla now lives in a place like Rivendell—only better.

And a massive library exists there. "Books in Heaven?" you might think. Yes. Even books about you and me and Kayla Marie Duerler. And I just wonder if this book you are reading right now is a glimpse of what her eternal book contains.

In the Bible, the apostle John wrote:

> And I saw the dead, great and small, standing before the throne, and books were opened. Another book was opened, which is the book of life. The dead were judged

according to what they had done as recorded in the books. Revelation 20:12 NIV

And Jesus said,

"The one who is victorious will, like them, be dressed in white. I will never blot out the name of that person from the book of life, but will acknowledge that name before my Father and his angels." Revelation 3:5 NIV

If You Only Read One Chapter . . .

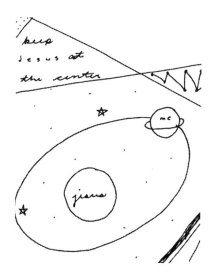

W hat really matters in life? What will last for eternity? I'm writing amidst the pandemic of 2020. The losses are stacking up. People all across the globe are losing their jobs, their hopes and dreams, and thousands upon thousands are losing their lives. It's incalculable. I think of Kayla's graduating class and how their expectations are turned upside down. No prom, no senior day, no normal graduation. This isn't easy.

If nothing else, the entire planet woke up to the fact that our earth-ly pleasures can be removed without warning. Sports cancelled. Performances postponed. Disney World closed. Malls vacant. Basics scarce. And the scariest thing is another global crisis could happen and be even worse. All of our "gods," the things we value so much, are failing us.

These disappointments can cause us to cave to depression, fear, and anxiety. Or we can shift our hope onto something that cannot be taken. We need a true God and a secure hope. If Kayla were still on earth, I believe she would not have been afraid of all that is going on. Kayla had this security. She had a rock-solid, hope-filled relationship with God.

I want to share with you how her faith developed over the years. One of her peers said, "If any of us were ready to go to Heaven, it was Kayla." Even though she didn't know when her time was coming, she was prepared. I hope this chapter inspires you to sink your roots deep into God's love so you won't be shaken by threatening events on this planet and, mostly, so you will be ready when your time comes to stand before God.

Just weeks before she passed, Kayla underlined this sentence in *Crazy Love*: "I am thankful for the unknowns and that I don't have control, because it makes me run to God."

In that same book, she read the chapter, "You could die before you finish reading this chapter." Kayla only made it to chapter seven (out of eleven) before it happened to her. But she was ready because she was surrendered to God and His will for her life. Here is the note she wrote to God before she started reading it.

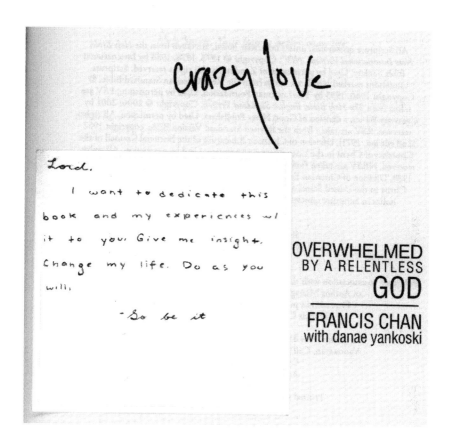

Crazy love

Lord,

I want to dedicate this book and my experiences w/ it to you. Give me insight, Change my life. Do as you will,

- So be it

OVERWHELMED
BY A RELENTLESS
GOD

FRANCIS CHAN
with danae yankoski

Her Faith in the Early Years

There is no way to count the number of prayers Jeff and I prayed for Kayla, but here is one I wrote when she was almost two years old, right before Rachel was born: "Lord Jesus, we love Kayla and Rachel so much! Please draw them to Yourself and place Your Spirit within them at a young age, and may they continue to grow and grow in wisdom and maturity. May they surpass us in their experience of You. In Jesus' name, Amen."

We are so thankful that she had a soft heart for God. She loved singing songs about Jesus as a tiny toddler, and she delighted to hear songs that spoke of His love for her. A dear friend gave Kayla a personalized album. "Kayla, you're precious in God's sight" is one line she heard often. This music spoke truth to her young soul.[6]

When Kayla was three, I wrote this in her memory book:

> When our friends were here, you initiated prayer before dinner. It was awesome. You included all the basic elements: thanking God, asking for his help, telling him you were glad we went to the water park and saying "He loves us" at the end. I cried with joy, and Daddy's heart leaped out of his chest!

Every time we put her to bed, we prayed with her and read from an age-appropriate Bible. We started very young with a book about the love Jesus has for children. When she was a little older, we read *The Jesus StoryBook Bible*.[7] This version showed Kayla that the Bible is not a book of rules or heroes, it is God's great rescue story.

The girls thrived on this Bible, and we had such fun reading it together. Usually, the four of us sat along the edge of Rachel's bed. When the following series of adjectives showed up (in almost every story), we said them in unison: "the never-stopping, never-giving up, unbreaking, always and forever love of God." Then Jeff stretched out his arms in front of us like the safety bar on a carnival ride, announced in a loud voice, "ARM BAR!" and gently shoved us backwards onto the mattress together. Wham! Then the belly laughs started.

---

[6] You can find the personalized music here: **bit.ly/MusicForChild**

[7] Sally Lloyd-Jones' children's Bible helps kids ages 4-7 (and the parents who read it) understand who God is, what He is like, and how much He loves us. **bit.ly/StorybookB**

When Kayla was five, she attended a day-long Christian camp. I wrote,

> It seemed as though that day changed you. You came back more mature. Since then, you've had greater control over your moods and attitudes. You said to me the next day, "Mommy, you don't have to give me timeouts for my bad attitudes anymore because I'm going to keep a good attitude."

Of course, she still struggled with bad attitudes from time to time, but it was wonderful to see her intention to overcome them.

When she was almost six, I wrote,

We just finished spring break. You have been so sweet-spirited. On Good Friday, I talked with you about what sins are and why Jesus died for us. You left the room, then came back a few minutes later. You asked me to guess what you did. When my series of ideas failed, you said, "I prayed and thanked Jesus for dying for me."

A few months later, when we moved to Harrison, Kayla explained she knew why—we were going to show people God's love by leading LifeSpring.

Elementary Years

While looking back at a language arts journal of Kayla's from first grade, I saw how often she focused her entries on God and her genuine love for Him. When most children are pumped about Santa or the Easter Bunny at holidays, this girl was excited about Jesus.

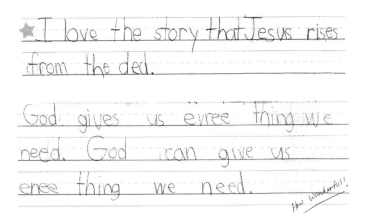

One night, Kayla's sensitive conscience got her out of bed. She needed to tell me her "sad" thought. She explained, "After playing Webkinz a lot today, I think my other pets are feeling neglected."

I responded, "Ok, then no Webkinz tomorrow, and you will play with your other animals." She liked that solution and went back to bed. I smiled, feeling glad that her sad thoughts weren't very sad.

On September 19, 2010, Jeff and I baptized her. She was beyond ready, but we wanted to make sure she totally understood the decision she was making. In her third grade year, she could articulate what she believed.

Conversations with Kelsey

I remember asking the girls about their faith and whether or not it was truly theirs or simply their parents.

Kayla said, "I don't feel there has ever been a time where my faith has been anyone else's but my own. I've always owned my faith."

Kayla memorized Bible verses to help her grow in her faith. I wrote to eight-year-old Kayla,

It's so awesome how you memorize Scripture! We have verses posted around your bed. Some of them are long, but you have each one memorized. I'm so excited for you! God will use those truths in your life in special ways.

Even from these early years, Kayla was Kingdom-minded and cared about people's souls. I remember one time I read this "conversation starter" and asked her to fill in the blank: "It makes me happiest to think about . . . ." I expected her to fill in the blank with "horses" or "Barbie and the Three Musketeers," her favorite things at that age. Instead, her response was, "It makes me happiest to think about all the bad people in the world accepting Jesus!"

When Kayla was eight I wrote to her,

> I love how your faith in Jesus is totally connected with the rest of your life. Lately as we are driving home from school, you have been showing Kennedy different things from the Bible, including John 3:16.

Kayla could have talked about anything during the carpool, but she actively shared her faith with her close friend. It was natural to her to include Jesus in daily conversations.

Around the same time, her grandparents took her to a state park where she played in the lake for a little while, then spent hours gathering rocks so that she could spell out "For God so loved the world" in the sand for others to see. She wanted people to know His love for them.

On our computer a few months ago, I discovered a page of verses that Kayla typed when she was ten. I was startled to see the same verse that Kayla was meditating on the week before the accident!

> The Lord is my strength and my shield; my heart trusts in him, and he helps me. My heart leaps for joy, and with my song I praise him. Psalm 28:7 NIV

Some might think the Lord *wasn't* her shield, that He didn't keep her safe, but He did. *He protected her soul.* He held her precious soul in His nail-scarred hands.

As you can see in another verse she typed that day, God protected her by giving her eternal life.

Kayla's Bible Verses

John 3:16 God so loved the world that He gave his only begotten son so that whoever believes in Him will not perish but have eternal life.

Psalm 28:7 The Lord gives me strength. He is like a shield that keeps me safe. My heart jumps for joy. I will sing and give thanks to Him.

Isaiah 41:10 Do not be afraid. For I am with you. Do not be terrified. For I am your God. I will make you strong and help you. My powerful right hand will take good care of you. I always do what is right.

In 2012, when Kayla was nine, I reflected on her legacy:

> I have been reading to you at night from our family's special books. They are biographies, written for children, about my grandparents, great uncles, and great-aunts who were missionaries to Asia in the mid-1900's. It's exciting to share this family history with you, and I'm even more excited to consider what God will do in your life—the legacy you will leave. I often pray Deuteronomy 30:6 for you and Rachel.

That verse reads,

> The Lord your God will circumcise your hearts and the hearts of your descendants, so that you may love him with all your heart and with all your soul, and live. Deuteronomy 30:6 NIV

I did not anticipate that she would leave before me or that I'd be a part of curating her legacy!

One summer day later that year, I asked, "Kayla, what would you say if I told you that Jesus is coming back this week?" With a huge smile she exclaimed, "I'd be so happy!" Her quick reaction brought tears to my eyes. I told her how pleased I was with her response, and she replied with innocent sarcasm, "What? Do you think I'd say, 'Oh NO!

I didn't do enough good things!?'" I chuckled and said, "You get it, don't you? You get grace." She said "yes," nodding with a knowing smile.

In her preteen years, she spent time with the Lord, using several devotionals, reading from her *Adventure Bible*, writing in a journal, and praying. She also thrived in the children's ministry at our church.

Teen Years

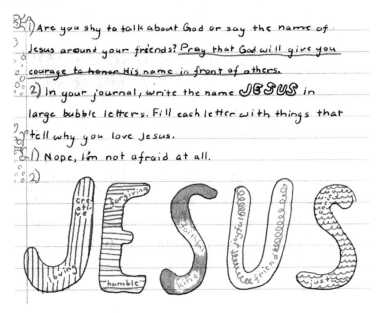

1) Are you shy to talk about God or say the name of Jesus around your friends? Pray that God will give you courage to honor His name in front of others.
2) In your journal, write the name JESUS in large bubble letters. Fill each letter with things that tell why you love Jesus.
1) Nope, I'm not afraid at all.
2)

On a beginning-of-the-year questionnaire in seventh grade, Kayla wrote "I love, love, love, love Jesus!" Then, that same first week of school, her teacher assigned each student to write a letter that she would send to them upon graduation. She wrote two. In this one, she asked herself many questions, then said, "I hope you have a good relationship with God." She closed the letter with "I'm praying for you."

She loved Aslan, the Christlike lion in the *Chronicles of Narnia* series. This attraction began in childhood and continued into her teens.

She named her stuffed animal lion "Aslan," wore an Aslan t-shirt, and had a wood-engraved lion phone case. In one of her YouTube videos, Kayla said the character she would most want to be with in an apocalyptic situation is Aslan because he's Jesus.

She drew this sketch with half a face. Interestingly, she owned a painting of Jesus that only showed half of His face. I was surprised when she bought it. We were in a bookstore, and I fully expected my book-loving daughter to use her gift card to buy books, but she saw that striking painting and knew that she had to have it. In her last uploaded video, she purposefully stood with His portrait right behind her.

Kayla was able to attend a Christian youth conference called MOVE in 2016 and again in 2018. Both experiences had a significant impact on her life. Kayla wrote about the lifelong commitment she made after the final session of MOVE 2016. The next entry shows her wrestling with feelings about returning home in a dialogue with her Heavenly Father. She wrote what she heard Him say (see asterisks). His silence about her specific role in the future is telling.

After Session 10:02

I rededicated my life to Jesus and committed my life to be a Kingdom Worker. This is a lifelong commitment. How will I stay connected to Jesus? * a long devo everyday

* get books on spiritual warfare

* pray

* worship

* serve

* memorize Scripture

What should I do when I grow up? Graphic design? Church work? I'm not being told anything. I'm willing to wait for it.

After Session

cont. 10:18 pm

Why didn't I feel anything when I read the letter? No joy, no love, no peace. I'm not looking forward to going home and I don't really want to see my parents or Rachel. I'm going to need a lot of help going back to old life. I am hesitant to be super changed because it will eventually fizzle out and I will go back to normal. It will remembered as the Love Stage, or the X stage where I was loving for a while. X

* It doesn't have to go back to normal.

I can be incredibly cynical.

* Don't be so hard on yourself. I love you. We can fix these problems. You have been made anew.

Am I witty? Huh. That's not one I would come up with.

I want to be wise again. I was not named Kayla for no reason. I have the capability to be wise, I just need to exersise it.

Jesus is the only constant.

After returning to regular life, Kayla wrote a letter to her "future self." She reminded herself why she chose to be a Kingdom worker and challenged herself to stick with it. She also instructed herself to not judge people at school, but to "Talk to them. Create a fellowship. Daily, build them up and encourage them."

Kayla often wore a wrench necklace. It said "Kingdom Worker" on it and was a symbol of her dedication to God and His plans. This dedication is why her friend Emma said, "Kayla truly inspired me to live ferociously for the Lord."

In the summer of 2017, Kayla and I went on a mission trip to Haiti. One of the leaders observed how often Kayla spent time writing in her journal. "You are always looking to spend time with Jesus, aren't you?" she asked. Kayla smiled, giving her a look that communicated "That's exactly it."

One evening during Kayla's last summer, while I was stretching on the floor, Kayla laid down next to me. We began to discuss the gift of speaking in tongues, something the Bible talks about. It was an ability she desired because of her passion for both languages and God. Although God has given me the gift of communicating with Him in this way, it is usually something I do when I am alone with Him, but I decided to pray in tongues with her that night since she was so hungry to know more. Her response was priceless. She was even more in awe of God over that gift than when He healed her friend's back injury right before her eyes.

One of the few verses Kayla underlined in the Bible is:

> "They will be my people," says the LORD of Heaven's Armies. "On the day when I act in judgment, they will be my own special treasure. I will spare them as a father spares an obedient child." Malachi 3:17 NLT

Kayla knew she was His treasure and that He wants everyone to be His treasure. She also understood the purpose of life: to accept God's love, love him in return, then love people and help them do the same.

everyone needs Jesus

∞∞∞∞

Just six months after she passed, we attended the memorial of a star football player in the next town who also died in a car accident. No one is guaranteed a long life in this broken world.

On 8-8-16, two years prior to the day of her home going, Kayla paraphrased the meaning of 1 Thessalonians 5:1-8 in one of her journals: "Jesus will come when we are least expecting it, but we won't be surprised when it happens. We are God's children, we know where we are going. That should affect everything we do—our entire lifestyle."

With the current world events, many are wondering if the end times are near. No one knows, but regardless, we need to be ready, like Kayla said. Our entire lifestyle should be affected. Whether we die or whether Christ returns, we need to know where we are going.

How about you? Do you have the security Kayla had? Do you have a rock-solid, hope-filled relationship with the God who loves you? Do you want to know Him better?

If you haven't already, I urge you to surrender your life to Him today. Think about this—Kayla never got the chance to finish the books she was reading that August. You may not have time to even make it through this book. Eternity is around the corner. For Kayla, it was a literal corner.

if you died today,
where are you going & why

Please take this opportunity to tell Him, "Lord Jesus, You value me so much that You paid the highest price to take away my sins so we can have a close relationship forever. I am sorry for my sins and turn from them to You. I accept Your gift of salvation, and I surrender to You. Make me Your own special treasure."

If you prayed this right now for the first time, you will find next steps in the epilogue.

Kayla and Me

I'm an affectionate person. My primary love language is physical touch. When the girls were young, I expressed my adoration of them with countless hugs and kisses. I was pleased when Kayla hugged me back at eight months. I recorded that moment in her memory book, along with other milestones, not thinking much of it. But then came Rachel. That girl snuggled from day one! I realized Kayla was not a physically affectionate person by nature, and I accepted that. She gave and received love in other ways, and she grew to be more affectionate.

When Kayla was two years old I wrote, "I made play-dough and fingerpaints from scratch. You enjoyed them so much, and after you finished many paintings, you spontaneously declared, 'I love you,

Mommy!' You understood that I made those things because I love you."

Before she turned three, there was a moment she astonished me with a mature response:

> I was frustrated with you because it seemed like you were deliberately moving slowly to the bathroom, and I ordered you to speed up. You responded, "I want to be a good girl. Mommy, will you be a good Mommy?" You melted me! I smiled, gave you a hug and apologized for being unkind to you.

I recorded the following story two days after her third birthday. It marks her attraction to rain from an early age.

> Dear Kayla, recently I took you with me as I volunteered at a church event. We were outside, and a strong storm kicked up. Tents were blowing across a field, lightning was striking nearby, thunder rumbled, and many kids were crying. You watched everything with your big eyes as I held you, but you didn't freak out. You and I even joked about the storm being like a big sprinkler with "boomies." I was so proud of your courage!

Kayla was not a very demonstrative child by nature, so I took it to heart when her little three-year-old self announced a heartfelt, "Mommy, I very, Very, VERY LOVE you!" as we were driving along one day.

When she was in second grade, I was recovering from major throat surgery and had to spend time away from home. To keep in touch, she and I sent e-cards because I was unable to talk without pain. One time she expressed, "I miss you so much I'm going to EXPLODE!" My homecoming was so sweet, and, for a few days she kept saying, "I'm so glad you're back!"—a sweet glimpse of the reunion to come.

My favorite stage of parenting was when she was a preteen. She was mature enough for more meaningful conversations but young enough to care about her stuffed animals like they were living.

For a while, our bedtime routine included her "talking" for her stuffed seal. She loved that creature so much, she considered it her own child. On my way out of her room, I called out in a sing-songy voice, "Goodnight Sealy!" Kayla ducked her head behind the white darling and replied in baby speech, "Goodnight Gwandma!" and then asked for a hug. As I hugged Sealy, I'd hear, "Awwww Gwaaaandma."

Love is spelled: TIME

Kayla's primary love language was quality time, but it was tricky because, as an introvert, she also needed alone time. Go figure! So I let her call the shots with how much time she needed. One way she enjoyed time "together" was for her to simply be near me while she was reading a book on her own. She was alone . . . but not alone. The perfect combo! Kayla spent hours on the chaise lounge in our dining room while I prepped meals in the kitchen.

As our relationship continued to develop, she grew more affection-ate. In her second grade journal, she wrote: "Winter is a time for snuggling. I like to snuggle with my mom." And she drew a picture of us side by side. When she was nine, we shared the warmest hugs, especially when I wore my thick, fuzzy robe. For some unexplained reason, she called me "Oobi" during that time. It was so endear-ing the way she'd say it, sometimes drawn out as "Oooobee" or when she would say, "Oobi, Nyah-Nyah, Mama." I revelled in these moments because she learned to savor closeness. In fact, she said one night, "I wish I could drink your hugs!" On another occasion I wrote, "You have been calling yourself the 'love sponge.' Last night you said that you wished there was an intercom so we could keep talking after I leave your room."

I recorded around the same time, "Kay Kay, I love you! I always have, and I always will. Lately you haven't wanted to grow up. You want to stay young so we can be tender with each other forever. But I assured you that hugs, kisses, and back rubs will always be available to you."

One evening she struggled to find the last word in a word search. She spent a long time looking and asked for help. When I found it, she declared that I won a lifetime supply of cuddles. She knew what made me happy.

Right after Kayla chose to be baptized in third grade, she went through a time of trouble. She didn't want to go to school anymore. She refused to get in the carpool minivan, and even when Jeff drove her, she still objected. There were a few days when her refusal was so strong that she was late to school. She was not a stubborn child, so we questioned her repeatedly. We were afraid she was being abused or bullied, but she insisted that nothing was wrong and that she just wanted to be with me.

We prayed about how to help her. After an enjoyable weekend together, we consulted with the school counselor and found a solution to get back to normalcy. Later, Kayla admitted the reason for her dread. She was distraught because she threw mulch at a boy and was disciplined (appropriately). She did not want to face those who were affected by her actions.

One December night, I threw my back out, and Kayla prayed for me as I put her to bed. Her compassion was a healing force.

I prayed for Kayla every morning as I spent time with the Lord. I used the book *65 Promises from God for Your Child*. As I continue to ask these appeals for Rachel, it's amazing to see how they were answered for Kayla. I praise God for being faithful. I also prayed *with* her every night and then again *for* her after she was asleep. I stood silently at the end of her bed, praying over her until I found out I was waking her. She told me she didn't mind because she felt loved and protected knowing I was there. To stop disturbing her rest, though, I began praying outside of her and Rachel's doors before I headed to bed.

One week during the summer when Kayla was ten years old, Rachel was with Grandma and Grandpa Duerler, so Kayla and I spent quality time together. One of the afternoons, she was eager to distribute door hangers from our church offering to pray for people's needs. During another afternoon, she and I made hair accessories. I remember working on them while swaying on the porch swing, talking, and enjoying one another's company. She enjoyed the rare opportunity of having me to herself.

On Rachel's ninth birthday, Kayla was so happy that she shared, "Sometimes I feel that we are the perfect family." I remember being surprised by that statement, knowing how imperfect our interactions were every day.

We had a splendid summer when she was eleven. One highlight was the week we pool-sat for friends on vacation. It was in a private setting, and we took full advantage of our time, swimming for hours each day and then coming back in the evenings with daddy for more fun. I set aside my "mom-hat," put on a ridiculous pink swim mask, and behaved like a kid with them. When I was a child, a chance to swim was like going to heaven for a few hours, especially because we didn't have air conditioning until I was ten. The girls and I did handstands in the shallow end, talked underwater and came up laughing, did backflips and forward flips underwater, dove for items at the bottom, rode noodle horses, did races across the length of the pool, played a million versions of Marco Polo with wackier word duos, came up with wild jumps off of the diving board, floated on rafts when we were tired, and ate snacks under the covered porch.

It was an absolute blast except for one frightening experience. Kayla dove ten feet to fetch a dive stick. She was without oxygen too long and when she emerged, panic covered her face as she gasped for air and struggled to stay above water. Thank God I was nearby, so I grabbed her and helped her to the side as she continued to choke and cough. I shudder to think if I was in the shallow end when it happened. We were terrified! Our precious girl had a close encounter with death that day, but it wasn't her time to go yet.

As the summer was ending, and Kayla prepared to start sixth grade, she had mixed emotions. She was afraid of transitioning to the school day. She enjoyed learning in a structured way, but she cherished being home. Many nights she was in tears about it. We prayed a lot together, and we watched her cling to God. She felt comforted by verses on hope that we printed and taped around her bed. The Lord gave her peace, and she was calm as she shifted back to school.

One winter day that year, Kayla, Rachel, and I made colorful clay charms for hours, and another time it was Shrinky Dinks. Exercising creativity was something all of us enjoyed. I brought home enormous sheets of cardboard from Sam's Club for us to paint and make backdrops for play times. I drew a basic setting, like a castle or a beach, and all four of us filled in the details. One time, I let the girls draw on their white socks with washable markers while they were wearing them. When Kayla was a preschooler, I allowed her to paint my face while Rachel took a nap. It stretched both of us out of our comfort zones, but it was bonding.

Other wonderful memories include the handful of snow days when I went into kid-mode again. I put on my winter gear and played outside with them, building forts, sledding, having snowball fights, hiking through the woods, making snow angels and letting the flakes fall onto our faces. I'm so glad I didn't send them outside to play without me.

But I wasn't a perfect mom, and I messed up plenty. I slipped this note under Kayla's door one night while she was sleeping:

> Dear Kayla, I'm very sorry that I was impatient and rudely cut you off when you were trying to think of the name of that Santa song last night. My impatience has hurt you many times and I deeply regret that. You are precious and valuable to me. Please forgive me for rudeness and impatience. Love, Mom

I wish I could recall all the conversations we had. She was easy to talk to and was open to my thoughts and beliefs. I remember how I prepared to have the reproduction talk with her when she was in fifth grade. I explained how God designed the physical "mechanics," why it is more than a physical act, and how it affects us spiritually. Her response surprised me. She leaned back with her hands behind her head and a contented look on her face and said, "I'm so glad you talk to me about things like this."

I don't remember what happened on Mother's Day when she was thirteen, but the following day, Kayla wrote this prayer to God.

> *Dear Lord,*
>
> *I'm sorry that I didn't try very hard to make mommy feel special. Thank you for her! Please show her how thankful we are to her.*
>
> *In Jesus' Name,*
> *Amen*

Later that year, I was amused when she said, "You're a good mom. You're not like those moms I read about in books."

After Kayla passed, I saw an application for the LifeSpring youth leadership team she had filled in as an eighth grader. Until I read it, I didn't know that she admired me and tried to be like me.

Who are the 3 most influential people in your life and why?

> The three most influential people in my life are Jesus, my mom, and my dad. I chose Jesus because he is the ultimate role model and I try to be like him. I chose my mom because I admire her and try to be like her. I chose my dad because he is another role model; he leads the church and has rental properties, worked on a paper for 12 years, and still has time for our family

I also found this entry from junior high on a day when I especially needed it. The verse was perfect, and her desire for me to have peace touched me deeply.

> ## Psalm 147:3
>
> He heals the brokenhearted and ~~the~~ binds up their wounds.
>
> Dear Lord,
>
> Thank you for giving me peace today. Please help me to do well on my tests today. Also, please help Mommy to have peace today.
>
> In Jesus' Name,
>
> Amen

Kayla and I were laundry-folding companions. We would dump all the piles on my bed then put on something to watch. She made tidy folded stacks of clothing while I shoved my pajamas into dresser drawers. One particular memory is the night we gently placed every clean sock on top of our purring cat.

It was easy to connect through our mutual love of pets. The more animals we gained, the happier Kayla became. One of our best-loved, spontaneous activities was sitting together showering adoration upon a furry member of the family, especially when Jeff and Rachel were there too.

Kayla never called me mom as a teen. She referred to me as "my mom," but when talking *to* me she preferred Mama, Mum (British style), or Madre (Spanish).

We didn't always get along. For example, I recall how frustrated she would be when I tried to help her study for AP Government. She requested my help and volunteered to wash dishes while I quizzed her, but I felt like I never did it right somehow. When we had conflict, we didn't always apologize. Love covered over the wrongs, but I was thankful for the entries I found where she talked to God about it.

> Dear Lord,
>   Thank you for Mommy! I'm sorry for getting angry at her. Please help me to control my anger.
>   In Jesus' Name,
>   Amen

When we journeyed to Haiti with other youth and parents from our church, we had separate experiences for the most part. I was proud of her for doing her job with excellence as the team photographer and for every time she played with the children (since she was not usually drawn to kids). My role was to pray for people and to talk with them about Jesus.

At the place we stayed, there were a few tense moments between us. For example, early one morning she was irritated when she thought "the moms" were waking the others too soon, but then she discovered the time on her phone was off by an hour. She also found it annoying every time I asked to borrow the SPF face lotion that I had assumed we would share. Then I felt frustrated with her at the start of the week because she didn't want to be social. She preferred reading while eating in a chair by herself. In hindsight, I should have realized that she was needing to recharge her introverted self because people constantly surrounded her. I'm so glad that during the last few days, the other members of the team convinced her to hang out with them.

We both enjoyed moments with the group singing "How He Loves" (which we sang at her memorial). Our most special moment together during the trip came when the ladies were slated to speak at a women's "conference." Picture a simple, large, cinder block open-air building, women sitting on benches holding babies, and kids everywhere. I relied on the Holy Spirit to give me words while I waited for my turn.

As I watched those mothers with their little ones, I felt inspired to share that Jesus loved blessing children, and I wanted to give them a practical example of how to do it. So I called Kayla up, joking about how she wasn't a little child anymore as she walked toward the front. I felt so much love and tenderness as I cradled her precious head in my hands while I blessed her with life-giving words. My friend, Linda, captured the moment. She gave the photo to me over a year after Kayla passed, and I cried as the memory came flooding back. It is our most cherished photograph of Kayla and me together.

Half a year later, during our last Christmas together, Kayla and I enjoyed a special day of shopping at antique stores. She wanted to hunt for a bookshelf, a genuine top hat, and old books. We found a green bookshelf that would match the mural she planned to paint on her wall, a vintage bowler hat, and some antique books. She also chose a copy of *Mere Christianity* by C.S. Lewis—not for its appearance but simply to read. The first woman who sold us books gave

Kayla an amazing discount because she was so impressed that a teenager liked antiques and reading so much. We were having so much fun on our hunt from store to store that we lost track of time and almost missed an evening Christmas service at our church.

The next week, Kayla invited me to help her paint the mountains on her wall. With her furniture pushed to the middle of the room and a newly adopted cat threatening havoc, we set to work. We had a joyful time listening to comedy as we brushed the scene. It was a wonderful experience laughing and painting with her. I love the sound of her laughter and cannot wait to hear it again!

Her final summer, I wrote her a letter. Before putting pen to paper, I once again asked the Holy Spirit to give me His words. I had no way of knowing this is the last blessing I would give her.

> May your relationship with the Almighty, All-Wise, All-Knowing, Brilliant, Majestic and tremendously loving and Holy God grow and grow and grow until you step into eternity and see Him face to face.
>
> I love you so much. I am so proud of you and I'm cheering you on! With intense "Momma love",
>
> Me

Now *she* cheers me on.

$\infty\infty\infty\infty$

As I share these vignettes from our mother-daughter relationship, I hope they spark love in your heart for your family. I pray you take advantage of every opportunity you have right now and that you focus on thankfulness for the time you had with any who are no longer here. If your childhood and family memories are especially painful, not joyous, I pray the healing love of the Father is poured into your life through the Holy Spirit.

Her True Self

Kayla knew *who* she was and *to whom* she belonged. This was the essence of her true self, as expressed by John Piper: "At the heart of what it means to be a Christian is to receive a new identity. In Jesus, we do not lose our true selves, but we become our true selves, only in him." Kayla decided to value what God thinks of her more than what people think of her. She became her true self by believing what He says. She blossomed in the warmth of His love.

Thoughts from Kelsey

As I was flipping through Kayla's copy of *Crazy Love* tonight, I saw she wrote, "I don't know what it's like to have a world without Jesus so how can I compare?"

I remember thinking when I was Kayla's age that I didn't have a testimony since I didn't remember a time without Christ. Someone once told me I should praise God for that BLESSING. He saved me before I even knew I needed saving. That is a beautiful testimony!

> I'm praising God that Kayla only knew a world with Jesus and will NEVER have to know a world without Him.

She created this document when she was in junior high.

You are fearfully and wonderfully made in God's eyes.

(Psalm 139:14)

You are the salt and light of the world in God's eyes. (Matthew 5:13-14)

You are complete in God's eyes. (Colossians 2:10)

You are loved in God's eyes. (Jeremiah 31:3)

You are worth delighting in. (Zephaniah 3:17)

You are forgiven and redeemed in God's eyes. (Ephesians 1:7)

You are anointed and have a purpose in God's eyes. (Isaiah 61:1)

You are beautiful in God's eyes. (Psalm 45:11)

You are more than a conqueror in God's eyes.

(Romans 8:37)

You are chosen, holy, and dearly loved in God's eyes. (Colossians 3:12)

You are God's handiwork. (Ephesians 2:10)

You are worth fighting for in God's eyes. (Exodus 14:14)

At the end of eighth grade, she wrote this letter to herself. She looked back and saw God's compassion and faithfulness. I'm still not sure why, but sixth grade was a lonely year at school. We prayed her through it and helped her cling to God's promises. We asked Him for friends she could connect with, and God answered.

Dear 6th grade Kayla,

   Would you believe me if I told you that you will become outgoing after two years at the junior school? What if I told you that you will end up with at least 10 friends?

   Kayla, would you doubt me if I said you would be involved in drama? Would you laugh if I told you that you will sing out loud!? Yes, it's true!

   Would you accept my statement that you will be able to do this: $\dfrac{\sqrt{4}}{\sqrt{24x^6}}$ or: $(x^2y^{16}z^{10})-(x^{12}y^4z)$?

Would you believe that you won't learn much in science? (Actually, you can probably believe that.) I bet you wouldn't be convinced if I told you that you will end up playing piccolo.

   Young child, you will become much more confident and unique. The trials you go through will make you stronger. Always remember this:

Jesus understands your struggles.

Love,
Kayla

I am a
friend
of ~~God~~

After Kayla passed, the high school dance coach was inspired by Kayla's understanding of her identity in Christ. When she heard the song, "You Say" by Lauren Daigle, she knew it would be a message Kayla would want them to share with others through dance. It reached thousands of people as the girls performed it at competitions in Kayla's honor. It's a powerful song about how God sees His children.

Here is what Kayla heard the Lord say to her specifically.

you are gentle

you are loved

you are secure

you are special

you are creative

you are my child

For an English assignment in tenth grade, Kayla wrote a description of herself called "I Am What I Am." In her brainstorming notes, she wrote the category "Faith" and underneath she listed these four things:

1. Peace in times of trouble
2. Self assurance
3. Not needing the approval of peers or adults
4. No fear of death

Here is how she put it together in one of her drafts:

"I am peace as it flows through my soul in times when it defies all logic. I am confidence because I know where my value lies. I am assurance in where I'm going after death. I am a child of God."

Kayla had everything she needed to be secure in life and in death.

Kayla's friend from Germany created a memorial video from this piece of writing. She had encouraged Kayla to stay involved in the BookTube community and to keep producing videos when Kayla thought about quitting. Thanks to May's inspiration, we have all of Kayla's YouTube videos to cherish.

bit.ly/MemorialBooktubeVideo

Like many people, Kayla was tempted to base her self-esteem on her YouTube channel's comments, views, and subscribers. You can see her wrestling with and overcoming feelings of insecurity in this prayer.

Dear God,

Thank you for my opportunity to be a part of the youtube community. Thank you for the equipment you've given me and the passions you've put in me. I'm sorry for putting too much of my value in views & comments & subscribers. It doesn't matter how many people know my name. Please help me shine a light in the youtube community. Set me apart from the nonbelieving crowd. Help me make a positive impact on my youtube community. Also, help me with consistency and uploading on time and on schedule. Thank you for caring about the smallest things in my life.

In Jesus' Name,

Amen

Kayla knew herself as God designed her.

I AM... clever
artistic
creative
wise
observant
humble
princess
aware
earth conscious

This is the only time I saw her write "princess." I like how she placed it after "humble." She knows that the King of Kings adopted her into His family.

> *"In Christ, we are fundamentally new. The language and values and customs and expectations of this world increasingly feel foreign to us. We have been born again for another world, to a greater kind of existence."*
> – John Piper

So she was.

So she is.

∞∞∞∞∞

Kayla's example prompts us to reflect on our own lives. Have I let God adopt me into His family? Am I daily choosing to live with a secure new identity that is not based on what *I* do but on what *He* has done for me and on whom He created me to be?

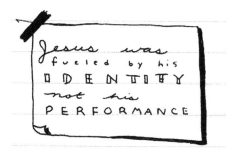

On a personal note, I needed this chapter as I edited it. My self-esteem plummeted this afternoon when I read an inspiring and beautifully written Instagram post by a musician who also lost a child. At the moment I read it, she had 444 "likes." My heart sank as I compared my seemingly "lame" voice to hers. I knew better than to slip down that path, but I let those feelings saturate my soul for awhile.

Comparison is a thief, an identity killer, and I recognized its cruel tone in my head. Jeff also noticed I was struggling. So we took a walk along a wooded path near our house. Kayla would have liked the location we chose with the sun filtering through the branches warming our skin, the birds chirping all around, and her favorite cat beckoning us to pet him. As it turned out, Jeff was feeling low about himself, too. We want so much to impact this world for God, but sometimes it seems our efforts fall short. Roadblocks, tech issues, lack of availability from others, fatigue, discouragement, and all the loss we're experiencing from the COVID crisis is starting to catch up . . .

We prayed and told God how we were feeling. The sky didn't part and angels didn't descend, but we felt the heaviness lift. After Jeff helped me dig up some wild onions, I washed the mud off with the hose and thought back to the year Kayla wanted to become a homesteader. She, too, dug up wild onions from the yard, but she dried them in her room and learned the hard way (from the smell) never to do that again!

A smile crossed my face. My mind filled with what she would say to me about my earlier self-doubt. I started hearing Kayla's voice encouraging me through the words of this chapter. I needed every one of them for myself, personally, today. I was touched as these truths led me back to *my true self.*

The mind *feasts* on
what it *focuses* on.
What consumes my
thinking will be
the *making* or
the *breaking* of
my identity.

Quote from *Uninvited* by Lysa TerKeurst.

Daddy's Girl

From the beginning of her existence, Jeff was smitten. His mini-me in female form came into being, and they just "got" each other. In Kayla's eyes, he could do no wrong—or almost no wrong. She respected him and valued pretty much everything he said to her. She was like a sponge when he taught her anything like chess or video editing or especially spiritual truth. Much of what she journaled came straight from his mouth, mainly through his sermons at LifeSpring. I believe that her genuine love for her Heavenly Father stemmed from her relationship with Jeff and how well he represented God to her. She called him "Daddy" to the end of her time on earth.

ABBA
"daddy"

When Kayla was born, we didn't know if she would be a boy or girl, but we were excited to raise the child God gave us. Having two brothers, Jeff was moved to tears at the wonder of having a daughter—a daughter! He adored Kayla as a baby, but, like many dads, wasn't exactly sure what to do with her. His specialty was giving her "airplane rides" by placing her over his forearm and cradling her tiny chin between his fingers. He would pray for her and bless her as he "flew" her around the house or yard.

Jeff was on constant lookout for ways he could contribute to her happiness. When Kayla was old enough to sit in an ExerSaucer, there was one little gadget that frustrated her. It spun, but could not be removed. I remember the night he got out his tool kit and disassembled that spinning wheel. We couldn't wait for her to discover that it was loose.

That was one of many times Jeff did something special for Kayla, no doubt inspired by his own mom's creative parenting style. Kayla's first "big girl" bed was a replica Conestoga wagon Jeff built, and she had a hard time parting with it later on. She beamed when she wore her one-of-a-kind eagle Halloween costume designed by her dad and made by them together. Later on, in junior high, he took her around town to military stores to find just the right wool army blanket to turn into a Middle-earth cloak.

Making things for and with Kayla was not the only way love flowed between this dad and daughter. Every night Kayla insisted on a special routine of putting her to bed. She never outgrew it, and Jeff shared special moments with her including her final night. In one of her BookTube videos, Kayla went on record saying her favorite "bookish" memory was when Jeff read to her every night into sixth grade. Fantasy was their favorite—the Chronicles of Narnia, the Chronicles of Prydain, then Tolkien's classics.

He was such a fun dad. He played with the girls, took an interest in what they cared about and were into, and helped bring out their wild side. He set up zip lines, tree swings, and water slides in our yard that kept them physically active and adventurous. Providing these kinds of opportunities was good because they were both naturally timid.

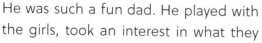

Another example: when they were still very young, he took a huge appliance box, flattened it, and set it up to create a "rocket" slide on a big armchair. Our little girls squealed with joy as he sent them down that short slope again and again. Then with a different box on a flat rolling dolly, he placed the girls inside and took them on a wild ride on the sidewalk. They delighted in the thrill of adventure within the safety of their daddy's strength.

When they were three and five, we have fun footage of Jeff propelling the girls in the air onto Rachel's full-size bed. Each toss had a distinct flair and a title. One of their favorites was "plate," which became the name for the game. One at a time, he positioned the girls horizontally on a pillow like they were being served on a plate and then launched them spinning into the air and onto the soft bed. They were insatiable, and Jeff kept entertaining them way past his point of fatigue. "New one, Daddy, new one," they cried: jackhammer, elephant, fork, roller coaster, flipsy-daisy. His creativity in hilarious tosses seemed to have no bounds until there was the inevitable oops moment when Kayla landed on her head. It was another close call.

Jeff and I valued taking videos of special moments. Before smart phones were a thing, we recorded experiences onto little DVR tapes. The spring of 2018, in the nick of time, I felt the urge to have them made into DVD's. We enjoyed watching them *with* Kayla the summer before she passed. I'm so thankful we had this opportunity to "relive" her childhood *together.*

When Jeff started his position with LifeSpring, Kayla had a front-row seat to watch her papa use and develop his leadership skills as he went from being a part-time interim minister to eventually being the senior pastor. Kayla wrote about her father in this loving essay.

Kayla Duerler
TAG 7
10-12-14
Leadership Essay

Leadership is about taking responsibility, not making excuses. My dad rarely makes excuses. Leaders are hardworking, and they teach others to be the best that they can be.

Father works very hard. He doesn't stop until the job is done. Working on a dissertation for 12 years takes perseverance, The dissertation was on the significance and role of olfaction in the ancient near eastern world, so Dad was translating Acadian text to English. My father owns and manages 30 rental units, never leaving a toilet clogged or a wall unpainted. Some days Daddy will be working on 1 unit for 7 hours! It can be hard on our family when he comes home at 10:00 pm, but we support him.

Leaders don't just tell people what to do, they teach the why and how of the doing. *So important*

Dad is a teacher. When I'm having troubles, Daddy teaches me what the Bible says about my situation. When I was going into 6th grade, I was very worried that I was going to miss my mom. I was so upset that I couldn't fall asleep at night. My mother and father were getting concerned, so my father decided to find some Bible verses to put on my bed that had to do with banishing fear. We found some good ones and hung them on my bed. Every night I would read a couple before bed. After that, I had no worries about 6th grade. After my dad gives the sermon on Sunday, members of *LifeSpring* say that he isn't preaching, he's teaching. *Great compliment* Preachers yell at others, teachers explain it to people in a way that they can understand. I have learned a great deal from the Sundays when my dad is teaching the Bible.

My dad is a leader to me. He teaches others to be the best that they can be and is hardworking. I'm inspired by the way my father lives his life.

Kayla was always willing to help her dad with projects around the house—planting grass seed, pulling weeds, washing the car, organizing his tools. She even went with him to work on a couple rental properties.

She also helped with ministry events. Jeff is involved in the local organization called This City His City. Most years they put on a powerful Good Friday event at the high school's activity center. Part of this experience was a station where participants walked through the garden where Jesus prayed the night before he was crucified. Kayla helped by hand lettering the standing signs. That was her last Easter weekend with us.

When Kayla was thirteen, she wanted to raise chickens. To get funding from us, Jeff required her to create a business proposal. Jeff was so smart to help the girls think through actions and the ramifications of those actions. He was definitely planning to get his girl what she wanted, but he didn't tell her until after she had thought it through. Together, they designed and built a mobile, raccoon-proof coop.

When the girls were twelve and fourteen, Jeff and I wrote notes to the girls every day in February leading up to Valentine's day.

OUR KAYLA

ONE OF THE THINGS JULIE AND I HAVE BEEN STRUCK BY IN YOUR LIFE IS YOUR LOVE FOR OTHERS AND THE WORLD. IT MANIFESTS IN YOUR COMMITMENT TO BE LOYAL TO YOUR FAMILY AND FRIENDS, TO PRAY FAITHFULLY FOR THE LOST, AND TO DESIRE FOR OUR WORLD TO BE REDEEMED AND RESTORED. THIS MAY BE, AT ITS ROOT, THE PUREST ESSENCE OF THE HEART OF GOD. TO SEE IT EVIDENT SO STRONGLY AT THIS AGE IS SOBERING. GOD MUST HAVE REALLY BIG PLANS FOR YOUR LIFE.
WE ARE CHEERING YOU ON, DAD+MOM

- SWIMMING UPSTREAM
- COUNTERCULTURAL
- UNAFRAID TO FOLLOW JESUS
- UNSTOPPABLE, UNWILLING TO ACQUIESCE
- BOLD AND COURAGEOUS
- FREE FROM PEER PRESSURE
- HUNGRY FOR GOD AND HIS HOLINESS/PURITY

THAT'S KAYLA DWELER.

WE ♥ YOU AND ARE PROUD OF YOU

DEAR KAYLA

HOPEFULNESS – I SEE THAT QUALITY IN YOUR LIFE. EVERY DAY YOU GET UP ON YOUR OWN WITH CONFIDENCE TO FACE WHATEVER CHALLENGES ARE COMING YOUR WAY. YOU OVERCOME ANXIETY, TRUSTING GOD TO WORK IT OUT — WHETHER IT'S SCHOOL OR A COMPETITION OR A RELATIONSHIP CHALLENGE. I KNOW YOUR HOPE COMES FROM GOD NOT YOURSELF, AND THAT IS SO INSPIRING TO US ALL.

LOVE YA, DAD

Hi Kayla

You, my lady, are such an amazing servant. You've always been helpful, willing to pitch in, even when not asked — whether it's bringing in the groceries or cleaning up the house or even working in the yard. I see the character and ministry of Jesus Christ alive in you, and it is a huge blessing to this world. You will never regret a single second of serving when we're in heaven someday. BTW, could you go pick up the kitchen table? Just kidding!!! ♡ you, dad

Driving the girls to school for the last two years of Kayla's earthly life was a bonding time. Kayla was a somewhat chatty morning person, so they'd observe little details about the route, or Jeff might pose a thought-provoking "what if" question to help Kayla develop a greater imagination or philosophical mindset. The route always ended with a prayer for them before they got out of the car. The content was often simple and always full of purpose: "Father, thank you for _____"—filling in the blank with whatever aspect of His nature they might have been aware of that morning. He prayed for God's blessing and empowerment, that the girls would know, love and serve Jesus that day. Specific names of friends were often featured. They prayed for the school, the teachers, the administrators, and the other students, especially the kids who were hurting and lost.

As she grew older and more independent, he struggled to let go, as many parents do. Just three months before Kayla passed, Jeff typed and printed a letter to each of the girls. He longed to have the best relationship possible with them, and he kept trying when it wasn't easy.

Dear Kayla,

I want to make sure I share my heart because it may not have been clear the other day at dinner. I was trying to be vulnerable, to let you guys know what I was going through so you could help the situation. I apologize and ask your forgiveness if I said anything that made you feel crummy.

As I mentioned, I've been getting hammered by negative thoughts about one aspect of our family—our time together. I feel like I was a rock star dad in a bunch of areas when you guys were young, but over the past few years, our family time has been a weakness, though it's not because I haven't wanted or tried. I want to succeed in our relationships at home like I want to succeed in every other area, so it's been tough feeling like I can't.

I think some of this is spiritual warfare directed at breaking down our relationships with each other and with God. I also think we have different expectations about what is important or ideal. And, not to throw out the proverbial "teenage years" thing, but I remember how tough it was for me when I was fourteen to sixteen, so I know that's a factor too.

What I didn't communicate is how hard I'm fighting these negative thoughts and feelings. I am clinging to these truths:

1. I love you. I love both you and Rachel more than any written or spoken words can articulate. It's really important that you both know that. This is the deep, underlying truth that doesn't change no matter how good or bad things seem to be going. I also believe you guys love me even when it doesn't feel like it. I appreciate all the ways you've communicated that over the years.
2. You are awesome. You are such an incredibly special person. You have a really striking blend of gifts and abilities and interests and passion areas. You've worked really hard to excel, but even if you fall short of your own standards, you stand out.
3. I am proud of you. We are honored to be your parents and are so proud of you. I thank God that you are making so many good decisions, ones I probably don't even know about.

I've been thinking about the helpful feedback you and Rachel shared about some practical ways we can connect as a family. Your idea to spend more time "hanging out" around the house vs. everyone isolating is a good one. Rachel mentioned how she appreciates opportunities to travel somewhere nice on vacation. This was a helpful reminder not to back off doing a vacation because we have so many animals to take care of, money is tight, etc. I will be praying about what that might look like for us this summer.

Our family is strong in many ways, but there is always room to improve. I'd like to hear your thoughts on any other ways I haven't mentioned that I could be a better father, so feel free to let me know if anything comes to mind.

Love you lots,

Dad

Thankfully, we had two really great vacations after that. I should mention our church was in a building campaign at that time, and we felt led by God to sacrificially invest over and above our regular giving. Jeff handles the finances, mostly, so he said we would probably need to cut out a summer vacation because of the cost. However, he clearly heard God tell him not to do that. Now, we look back with grateful hearts because we have those experiences to cherish for the rest of our days.

First, we went to our friends' lake house in Tennessee. We played games galore and explored the area on their boat. There was a special bonding moment when he and Kayla swam to shore, fending off a water snake, and ascended a rock precipice to jump off. He found a good spot lower down for her, then headed to the top. Surprisingly, Kayla followed him higher and jumped with him.

Kayla was becoming quite the adventurer. From that same trip, he cherishes the memory of scampering down many flights of stairs in the dark to jump in the pitch black water to cool off after boiling in the hot tub.

One month later, we traveled to New Jersey and New York to celebrate Kayla's sixteenth birthday. A highlight for Kayla was seeing one of her favorite musicals, *The Phantom of the Opera*. Before the show, Kayla was admiring the overpriced fan swag, especially a zip-up hoodie. Jeff and I had the idea to get her something special to remember that day, so during an intermission, I snuck away to buy it from their souvenir shop. When we presented it to her that night, she was deeply touched.

It may sound like a small thing, but that $70 sweatshirt felt like an extravagant gift. We see her pleasure about it from her writings that night: "I felt so blessed. Gifts must be one of my love languages." She even kept the bag it came in, made a pocket for it in her journal, folded it neatly, and tucked it inside. Oh, how we wish we could pour out lavish love on her again now, but we hold on to the confidence that she couldn't be more satisfied by her Abba Father in the richness of Paradise.

Recently, Jeff answered an icebreaker question, "What is your dream job?" with "I'd rewind time and be a stay-at-home dad to have more time with Kayla and Rachel." There are times when we deeply feel the pain of all we have lost with Kayla's passing, but each time those feelings get replaced with the unshakeable conviction that the present can't even begin to compare to what we will experience together in eternity.

And so there is a peace that is even greater than the pain. For Jeff's first birthday without Kayla, I had a necklace made with her fingerprint on one side and Kayla's handwriting on the other: "Peace be with you, Daddy." He wears it every day.

∞∞∞∞

"The intense love of a human father is but a glimpse of the Heavenly Father's love." That sentence introduces a moving video Jeff made a couple months after the accident.

bit.ly/mydaddylovesme

The video captures clips and photos of Jeff and Kayla starting near the end of her life and reversing to her birth. The song Jeff set it to ("Embrace" by Jake Hamilton) voices the longing we all have for the Heavenly Father's loving presence. When paired with images of Kayla and Rachel lighting up their daddy's eyes, it's a tangible reminder of how God views us.

As the song goes on, it echoes this refrain, "And I don't wanna wait to go to heaven when I die, I'm gonna go right now." The love of God is not just a future hope, it's meant to be a present reality. "'This is the sound of Heaven invading Earth," Hamilton belts out.

I imagine this "sound" to be the glorious chorus of children squealing with delight and laughing as they play with their strong, safe, loving Father.

"Again, Daddy, again!"

Concern For the World

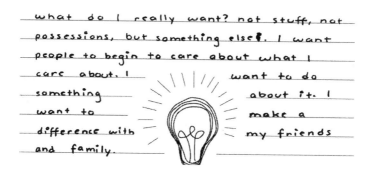

what do I really want? not stuff, not possessions, but something else?. I want people to begin to care about what I care about. I want to do something about it. I want to make a difference with my friends and family.

arly on, Kayla cared about matters beyond herself. She noticed the brokenness of this world. She wanted to help and make a difference. In her first grade school journal, she expressed her desires and concerns.

I am a good citizen because I rlly rlly want to pick up trash!

Good for you!

Eight-year-old Kayla wrote to our local newspaper about the excessive litter that she noticed in certain areas of our town, and she even listed action steps the community could take to fix the problem.

Dear Editor,

My name is Kayla and I am 8 years old. I'm concerned about the trash I see in Harrison. One day I counted 373 pieces of trash on the side of the road as I rode home from school in the bus! And that was just on one side of the road!! I wish people wouldn't litter because it pollutes the earth and it looks horrible!! It's really bad on New Biddinger and along the fence near Exit 1 and probably lots of other places too. Instead of throwing trash out of a car window, people can put bags in their car to put trash in, then throw it in a trash can at home or put recyclables in a recycling bin. All it takes is a few simple shopping bags in your car that you can put wherever you can reach. I hope the people of Harrison will stop littering. It would be nice if people would pick up the litter that is already on the ground (and in the trees and bushes) too. My family and I are going to participate in the Great American Cleanup in Harrison. If anyone else would like help, please contact cleanupHarrison@gmail.com.
It is taking place April 16th from 10am-Noon.
Here's the website for Keep America Beautiful
http://www.kab.org for great ideas too.

Thank you,
Kayla Duerler

The next year, she took further action, which I included in her memory book:

I love your good heart, Kayla! Lately, you have been wanting to collect and save money to give to the poor, and at school, you gathered papers from the trash cans so you could bring them home to recycle them. The next day you took a paper bag to school so students would separate their papers from the garbage.

At the same age I posted to Facebook: "You know your child has truly gone 'green' when she insists on recycling a single staple. 'But Mommy, they can melt it down and reuse it!'"

As a preteen, Kayla spent hours on Freerice.com answering questions to earn grains of rice to feed the hungry. She was determined to make a difference, one miniscule seed at a time.

Inspired by the book *A Long Walk to Water*, Kayla made a logo and sold her handmade embroidery thread bracelets. She gave every penny of her earned money to help build wells in Swaziland through her aunt and uncle's medical partnership with the Clean Water Foundation.

Not stopping there, she sacrificed her small savings to our friends who were running a marathon to raise money for Team World Vision to bring clean water to Africa.

WEARABLES
>>>>>>>>>>>>> *for* <<<<<<<<<<<<

WATER

PROCEEDS PROVIDE CLEAN WATER FOR PEOPLE IN AFRICA.

Every Christmas, she wanted to receive gifts purchased from ethical brands or from organizations that support a good cause. For example, I gave her a jewelry box made of upcycled glass bangles that supported women artisans from India. In it, Kayla kept a MudLOVE bracelet from her grandparents, which helped provide someone in the world with clean drinking water. Her final Christmas present to me was homemade reusable kitchen wrap. She bought fabric, cut it into various sizes, then coated them with melted beeswax.

As a teen, she declared in her writings "[I am] joining God in loving the earth he has created. This is what I'm PASSIONATE about." She convinced me and many others to stop using Google as our search engine and to use Ecosia.org, instead, because they plant one tree for every forty-five searches.

She was conscientious to conserve water and electricity as much as possible. I always knew when she was brushing her teeth (with a bamboo toothbrush and clay-based toothpaste) because I heard the faucet turning on and off. She used only what was necessary.

Kayla also tried to limit her use of the space heater, even though her bedroom is located on the lowest floor of our home where the temperature drops more than the rest of the house.

I have to say, as hard as the COVID-19 crisis has been, Kayla would be pleased that air pollution dropped as much as 60% in major cities according to IQAir.

All of God's creation mattered to Kayla, especially animals. She became a vegetarian when she was fourteen to protect animals from mistreatment in the meat industry.

One summer afternoon, we were approaching our exit on the freeway when a semi-truck full of cages passed us. It was loaded with mishandled turkeys heading for slaughter. The still-living, white birds were already bloodied. My heart sank, and I glanced at her horrified expression. Kayla took photos of the turkeys as the truck drove by so she could bring greater awareness to this cruel practice. Then she buried her face in the crook of her arm and cried the rest of the way home. Kayla couldn't stand the mass killing of any creature.

In her last two years, she became a minimalist and shopped at second-hand stores because of her concern over the unethical treatment of fast-fashion laborers. She desperately wanted to make a difference in this area of injustice. Kayla led classmates in discussions and debates and influenced them to shop consciously too.

sustamability

- zero-waste
- fashion
- child labour

While watching a "fast fashion" documentary, her heart broke over the loss of many people in a garment factory collapse. Even though the clothing companies knew the conditions were unsafe, they did not protect their workers. She hated how the laborers barely made a living wage, and she felt frustrated over the lack of employment options for people in impover-ished nations. As best as she knew how, she fought for the less fortunate by using her purchas-ing power and avoiding problem retailers.

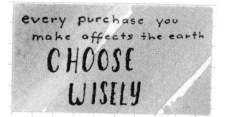

every purchase you make affects the earth

CHOOSE WISELY

On March 14, 2018, her zeal to support innocent victims led to her participation in the Enough! National School Walkout. This was the response to the school shooting that killed seventeen students in Parkland, Florida. It caused controversy among parents, teachers, and students across the United States and within her own high school, but Kayla wanted to honor the lives of those who died. She was sitting in one of her toughest classes when the moment came for her to leave the room. Sensing the absence of approval from her teacher, she bravely left the classroom and the building.

When Kayla cared about an issue, she was willing to advocate for it even in the face of disapproval. Once she reached the location where the seventeen-minute gathering took place, Kayla wasn't passive. She and her friends took action by praying together and taking their concerns to the One who can heal hearts and change lives. They prayed for the end of school violence.

∞∞∞∞

There are so many problems in our world, but God has a calling for each of our lives. Through these little drawings, Kayla asks us to reflect on the needs of this world. She would want each of us to research and be part of a solution to at least one problem that we really care about.

Core Values and Life Goals

meraki - (v) to do something with soul, creativity, or love; when you leave a piece of yourself in your work.

When Kayla was in seventh grade, she wrote a list of five things she wanted or hoped for more than anything. When I was in seventh grade, my list would have been very different than this. Even now, I am challenged by her desire for humility.

1) Be as honest as you can, think of five things you want or hope for more than anything and write them in your journal.

1) Five things:
- God
- a good life/future
- compassion
- humility
- purity

Kayla's values guided her goal making.

1. lead many people to Christ & help them stay there
2. live a healthy, zero-waste lifestyle
3. disciple / mentor people
4. develop a selfless mindset
5. have a job that is what I love & serving God.

We are thankful that her top goal is being accomplished even though she's not here.

On summer break when the girls were younger, they had to follow a few daily rules before watching anything on a screen. The hope was to help them become productive, not entitled. When Kayla entered high school, they had more freedom over how they spent their time, but Kayla continued the tradition on her own. She even practiced self-control during a winter break with the following rules:

1. No computer in the first two hours of the day
2. Practice at least once a week (flute)
3. No more than two movies in one day

She constantly kept her goals and plans in front of her. I did not count them all because it's overwhelming, but it looks like every single day of her last two years has its own to-do list.

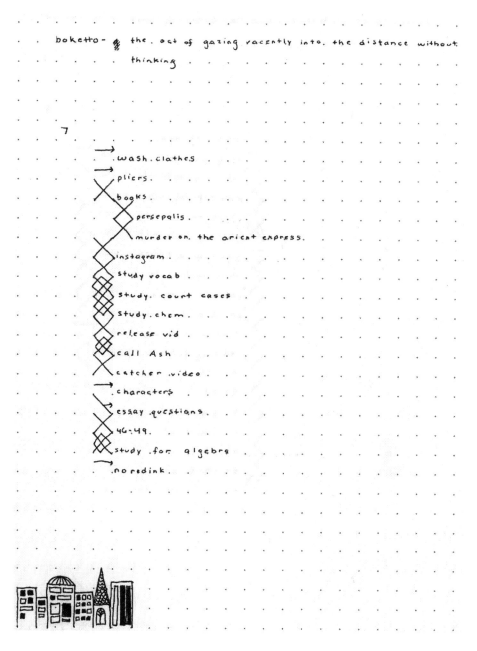

boketto - ✻ the act of gazing vacently into the distance without thinking

7

→ wash clothes
→ pliers
✗ books
◇ persepolis
murder on the orient express
◇ instagram
◈ study vocab
◈ study court cases
◈ study chem
◇ release vid
◈ call Ash
✗ catcher video
→ characters
◇ essay questions
◈ 46-49
◈ study for algebra
→ no redink

Productivity is a value that she embraced, but she also planned plenty of fun and tried to set aside one day per week when she was more restful than the others.

Here is her summer wish list.

I WANT TO:

watch Little Dorrit
read Percy Jackson
buy a patch for backpack
wear POTO jacket on first day of school
get driver's liscense
make stickers for back to school
record one second a day
write a sentence every day
print summer photos
knit a scarf
hydrogen peroxide hair
see Kendall every day
read Brave New World
finish Girl Meets World
knit a sweater
watch on Avengers movie every month
go on college visits
photoshoot w/ guard
work on jean jacket
go to marching band competitions
meet Caitlyn
go to Coffee Peddlar for a study session
go to library after school
get together w/ friends for Halloween
make finals in marching band
paint
work on Redbubble artwork
get new phone

Kayla was strategic and made all sorts of plans for her last summer. In addition to reading, filming, and making art, she also thought ahead to marching band season.

MARCHING BAND
——— p l a n n i n g ———

show name -

music - Connections by John Zannun

my job - attendence : make sure people are in the
right place at the right time

DON'T BE UPTIGHT !

what to do

I need something to record when people will be
gone and daily attendence   Maybe a notebook?

& I need a roster so I have all the names

Find band hairstyles

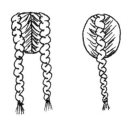

fun - one sec of footage every day

ESCAPE THE ROOM

Health was important to her, so she tried to treat her body as the temple of the Holy Spirit. She wanted to be able to make ten dinner meals and five breakfasts meals, try diverse food, shop on her own, go to the international section of the grocery store, and make her own bread. She even planned to drop sugar for a while, but I don't think she did it for long. That's a hard one!

In 2017, she kept track of character goals. For example, September was peace, and January was joy. She created a grid and put a dot on every day that she felt she practiced that quality. Here are her over-all goals for that year.

Datum / Date:

2017
goals

a bad habit I'm going to break: *Cracking my knuckles*

a new skill I'd like to learn: *spinning a sabre*

a person I hope to be more like: *Jesus*

a good deed I'm going to do: *be kind to my family*

a place I'd like to visit: *Haiti*

a book I'd like to read: *Sherlock* √

a letter I'm going to write: *to RG & Lizzie* √

a new food I'd like to try: *vegan & vegetarian meals*

I'm going to do better at: *being loving*

one word: AWARE

The next year she trimmed her goals and yet made powerful declarations.

IN 2018

I will be stronger, braver, kinder and unstoppable.

One of her friends said "determination" stands out when she thinks of Kayla. When she wanted to do something, Kayla didn't stop working until the goal was accomplished. But it wasn't always easy to stay on task. In her last month of life, she asked God for motivation. She wrote in a prayer,

I have a lot to get done and I need to want to do it.

I can feel the figurative weight piling up.

Then a few days later she said,

Thanks for giving me that first push and helping me stay motivated.

Her biggest heartfelt goals were to reach her friends with her Savior's love. Some ways she intended to do this were to share *The Bible Project* videos with Ashley, who had a lot of questions and doubts about God, and to give a "letter from God" to a hurting friend.

Kayla could have been successful in so many career paths. She had an amazing right/left brain balance that enabled her to be a creative artist yet excel in math and science. But it was her ambition for people to know Jesus that won the day.

In Haiti, while on a mountaintop overlooking a decimated valley, we took communion. Later that night, she recorded the experience:

> I feel a calling to help in missions whether it be in short trips or full time when I'm older. I also had a vision of Jesus' blood as rain washing away the garbage and pollution in Haiti.

The path she planned to pursue resulted from her love for the Spanish language and her heart for people. She felt called to become a missionary. Spain is a beautiful country, and she longed to live there, but not for personal comfort or a lucrative lifestyle—she wanted to lead the residents of Spain into a relationship with Christ.

spain notes
_____

Jesus earthquake- I won't do anything until I've created a
Jesus earthquake at home
in advance- research the problems
in spain
find a mission partner to pour
$ into
determine a way to fundraise
fundraise
pray
find colleges w/ exchange programs
missions-

GO→

A few weeks after Kayla passed, a friend of ours who serves and speaks at a church in NYC shared about her life. The message was translated into Spanish for a segment of their population. A few young adults decided to be baptized because of her testimony. This helped fulfill Kayla's hope to reach Spanish-speaking people.

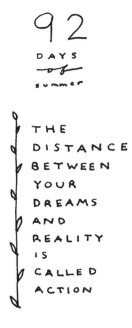

92
DAYS
~~of~~
summer

THE
DISTANCE
BETWEEN
YOUR
DREAMS
AND
REALITY
IS
CALLED
ACTION

In the end, there were only 68.5 days of summer for her. Even though she did not know that her life on earth was coming to a close, she spent her remaining moments accomplishing goals and making memories with friends and family. This is the way she lived her everyday life. Like time matters. Like time is limited. Like eternity is around the corner.

8

- ☐ finish lesson 4
- ☐ drive
- ☐ whap
- ☒ shower
- ☒ exercise
- ☐ read Brave New World
- ☐ chem
- ☐ edit video (ac)
- ☐ paint
- ☐ chores
- ☐ one second
- ☐ write thank you notes
  - ○ 1
  - ○ 2
  - ○ 3
  - ○ 4
  - ○ 5
- ☐ vacuum
- ☐ plant
- ☐ $$ talk
- ☒ clothing list

When I scanned her final to do list from the morning of the accident, the line "Read *Brave New World*" stood out to me. Instead of reading about another world that day, she entered a glorious one. Meanwhile, everyone who knew her entered a new world where we had to be brave without her.

As I flipped through the blank, never-to-be-filled pages of her homemade summer journal, I prayed, "Oh, Lord, please let there be one more thing." And there was! Amidst the remaining empty white pages, I found this little scrap from the book *Hawaii's Queen Liliuokalani*. Here's a verbose line that she preserved: "Liliuokalani was more than ever impressed with the magnitude of the high mission to which it had pleased God to summon her."

That little discovery felt like another confirmation that what is happening with Kayla's life now is supposed to happen. It comforts me, but it's more than that. God summoned her to live according to these goals and values—her life's mission, but it hasn't stopped. She continues to reach people even though He summoned her home.

Unstoppable indeed.

∞∞∞∞∞

If you, like me, want to be faithful to God's calling in your life, even if you aren't sure what it is, I invite you to join me in simply asking, "Father in Heaven, help me to value what You value and accomplish what You want me to accomplish for Your glory."

Sisters

As you will discover, Kayla and Rachel had a lot of fun together, but they also had some issues with sibling rivalry, personality clashes, and jealousy. Kayla wanted to be a loving sister, yet she sometimes struggled to be that way. Underlying their relationship, though, was a foundation of love.

I count it such a privilege to be the mom of these two precious daughters. Here are some of the fun and significant moments they shared. They are taken from the memory books I wrote to each of them.

The day after Kayla turned two, I propped Rachel, who was three months old, into a seated position. Kayla gave her hug after hug. Rachel was so happy that Kayla was giving her such warm, loving affection. Then, a few days later, I stood Rachel up after bath time. When she saw Kayla, she laughed her *first* hearty laugh, which made Kayla laugh, too. It was the first of many laughs together!

To Kayla, age two: "You're such a caring sister. You are protective of Rachel, always making sure that the gates at the staircases are locked shut and looking out for her other needs as well. You offer her toys, her blanket, and her bottle when she fusses. Rachel is blessed to have a big sister like you!"

I recorded the first time they played together. A few months after Rachel's first birthday, she was holding a cloth and started teasing Kayla by running away from her. Rachel always had a great sense of humor that showed up early. Kayla realized that Rachel wanted her to play, so she took hold of the other end of the cloth so that Rachel had to chase her. They both giggled and squealed as Kayla led Rachel around the house.

To Kayla, age three: "We were walking home from the park, you beside me and Rachel in the stroller. The sun was in her eyes, so I flopped her hat on her head. You noticed that the butterfly was not showing on the front. I said, 'It's okay, as long as it covers her head.' You said, 'I don't like it wrong; I like it right.' I smiled and said, 'Me too,' and turned her hat around the *right* way."

Also, when Kayla was three, I wrote: "I was so proud of you at the playground today. You were crying in my lap because you had just fallen and skinned your knees. The instant Rachel started to walk toward the parking lot, you immediately stopped crying, sprang up, and ran to stop her. You were more concerned for her than for your own comfort."

To Kayla, age four: "Last night, Rachel asked for you to put her to bed. 'Kaya put me bed?' was her exact request. She couldn't quite say the 'L' yet. You sang, 'Jesus loves me' to her then prayed a prayer that was many sentences long while placing your hand on her tummy."

The same year I wrote, "You know how difficult it is to get Rachel to eat her veggies, so every time she took a bite, you offered her one of *your* dried cranberries. We didn't ask you to do this, you just helped."

One day when Kayla was five, we were grocery shopping, and the girls ran down the aisle holding hands. A few minutes later, Rachel said to me, "Mommy, I want to be a big sister." I asked, "Why do you want to be a big sister, Rachel?" She answered, "Because I want to be like Kayla!"

To Kayla, age six: "This morning you and Rachel played together without one disagreement, which is rare. I caught some video of you scooping watermelon and singing songs together. It was cute because sometimes Rachel sang the wrong words, but she sang with total sincerity and confidence, and you didn't correct her."

To Kayla, age seven: "Right now you and Daddy are on vacation in Michigan with Grandma and Grandpa. Rachel and I stayed home because she gets carsick, and it is a nine hour drive. She and I were playing Go Fish when she started to say, 'I have more c-' She was going to finish with 'cards than you,' but she stopped and said, 'Oh, I shouldn't say that. That's bragging.' I was so impressed! Then she told me that before you left, you started to say to her, 'I get to go on sand d-' (dunes), but you stopped yourself and said, 'I shouldn't say that. It's bragging.' You set a good example for Rachel. Also, Rachel really misses you. She keeps accidentally calling me 'Kayla,' and she can't wait for you to come home to play with her."

One morning, Rachel wanted to use Kayla's markers that she received at a friend's birthday party, but Kayla was using them and didn't want to share. Rachel became upset, so Jeff tried to distract her by asking, "Rachel, how did you sleep last night?" to which she responded, "Terrible! I had a bad dream." We asked, 'What was your dream about?" She answered, "Kayla wouldn't let me use her markers!" We couldn't help but laugh at her clever reply.

A few months later, Kayla and I did a special shopping trip together, and I noticed how she mentioned Rachel many times during that experience. She wanted to include her even though she wasn't there.

When I pulled into a parking spot on a winter day, Kayla said, "Oh good! I love it when you park between two cars—it feels so cozy." And Rachel agreed wholeheartedly. It's interesting how they felt the same. There were other unique areas of sensory perception they shared, such as how numbers, letters, and names were color-coded in their minds. They didn't always agree on colors, but they had fun bantering about whether a *t* was green or blue, for example.

When seven-year-old Rachel was taking a bath, she declared that she was ready to get baptized. While she was in the tub, we had a good discussion that made it clear she was ready. Rachel asked if we could practice putting her under water. I added more water so it would be deep enough. But the suds turned into the best bubble bath ever! We weren't able to practice, but we could celebrate! I turned on the jets, and the bubbles rose over the rim of the tub. Kayla joined in the fun, and they had a blast making bubble hats on each other's heads and being silly.

To Kayla, age nine: "Yesterday, Rachel was baptized. You were so sweet and supportive, and you said to Daddy the night before, 'I'm so glad that our whole family will be in heaven together someday.'"

Baptism doesn't change the fact that people still struggle sometimes. Half a year later, Kayla wrote this New Year's Resolution.

My New Year's Resolution   Jan. 4, 2012
My New Years resolution is to be
nicer to my sister at home and at
school. I chose this resolution because I
know my sister and my mother will appreciate
it. First I will try to stop arguing with
Rachel on Mon., Wed., and Fri. Then on Tue.,
Thurs., and Sat. I will play with her very
nicely. Finally on Sunday I will try to be
all around nice to Rachel! My resolution
will bring more peace to our home. This
year I will try to be nicer to my sister!!

All four of us savored the moments of unbridled joy between Kayla
and Rachel. Like when they repeatedly slid down the carpeted stairs
on their bellies in their footy pajamas. Also, how they came up with
ridiculous combinations of dress-up clothes and recorded silly skits.
The holidays always made them giddy. Our favorite memories of
laughter and hilarity came from celebrating Christmas and Easter,
and they never needed to believe in Santa or the Easter Bunny to
make it fun.

There were certain songs that excited them, and they listened to the same radio station in their rooms when they were young. Whenever the song "Move" by MercyMe came on, Kayla would run to Rachel's room, and they would jump and dance on Rachel's bed together. Dancing was something that consistently brought them together.

When Kayla was eleven and Rachel was nine, they choreographed and performed a cute dance routine to "Welcome to the Show" by Britt Nicole. They wore clothes that glowed in the black light and used neon hula hoops and streamers as part of the act. They were the finale of "Harrison Kidz Got Talent" at our church. It was great to see them work together. Here is the performance in a fully lit room.

 bit.ly/neonroutine

To Kayla, age eleven: "Dear Kayla, I admire your maturity. You are always working on bettering yourself. Recently, I asked you to begin sharing the *American Girl Magazine* subscription with Rachel since she is now interested in it, too. You clearly didn't like that idea and stomped off to your room . . . but less than ten minutes later, you reappeared with an improved attitude and a practical solution that would satisfy you both. I was amazed and impressed!"

> Give me love. I can't love people on my own. I need your love for humanity. Help me love my sister.

When Rachel was eleven, we visited the National Underground Railroad Museum. It broke her heart to see that slavery still exists today. She decided to make felt frogs and sell fifty of them so that she could give money to the International Justice Mission. Kayla was excited about her project, prayed for its success, and took photos of the frogs to help her sell them.

In Kayla's application to become a student leader in eighth grade, the prompt told her to list some of her strengths and describe a time when she used them. She responded, "I'm very organized, patient, creative, and merciful. I was merciful when my sister and I had a big fight, and I forgave her very soon." Here is a picture that demonstrates how different they were *at the time.*

The scan below is from Kayla's 2017 summer journal. The girls were fifteen and thirteen. I love how God spoke to her, and she agreed with him.

When Rachel is being difficult, she is under attack. Pray for her rather than hating her, for you are under attack as well. It is part of the attack for you to become angry at her.

Señor,
    I'm sorry for hating Rachel yesterday. Thank you for speaking to me.

During the summer of 2018, the girls were struggling to get along even more than usual. I see in Kayla's prayers her desire for a good relationship but her struggle to make it happen.

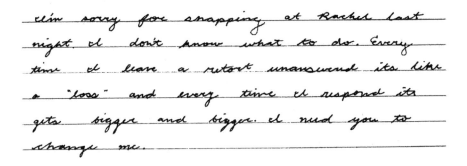

I'm sorry for snapping at Rachel last night. I don't know what to do. Every time I leave a retort unanswered its like a "loss" and every time I respond its gets bigger and bigger. I need you to change me.

In those last months, every night, I stood in the hallway, placing one hand on each of the girls' doors, praying for their relationship and for them individually.

We are thankful that Kayla wrote a heartfelt card to Rachel for her fourteenth Birthday (the last one together) expressing how glad she is that Rachel is her sister. She even loved her in Rachel's love language (gifts) by giving her money tied with a little string.

Now we know Kayla is loving Rachel perfectly from Heaven and cheering her on, while Rachel is cherishing memories with Kayla and trusting that she will see her again. It's heartbreaking and precious at the same time. Rachel has peace in her heart about where Kayla is, but she misses her, has dealt with regret, and has occasional dreams that Kayla returns. The permanency of an only sibling passing is a tough reality to face, especially as a teen.

Hundreds, maybe thousands of people were concerned and praying for Rachel. We are eternally thankful for every plea made on her behalf. God answered those prayers and sheltered her heart. She not only survived the huge loss, but she is thriving. God has surrounded Rachel with many friends. I have a feeling that Kayla is pleased with how Rachel has many good, caring, and fun "sisters." Even though they will never replace Kayla, they are a wonderful blessing.

∞∞∞∞

Sibling relationships usually have a mixture of joy and strife, so there's always room to grow. Perhaps you're in a struggle right now. If Kayla were here, she would encourage you to talk to God about the relationship and ask for His help. One key to having no regrets is to forgive.

One late night Kayla came to me because she was feeling bitter. I asked Kayla to be specific about everything she needed to forgive Rachel for doing or saying. I scribbled down the list as she thought of the offenses. Then I led her in a prayer of forgiveness for each one. Afterward we destroyed the list and Kayla felt relief. It helped her more quickly forgive when the next conflict came up because she wasn't holding a record of wrongs against her sister.

Is anything bothering you about a close family relationship? If so, you can find relief too. It might help to make a list of specific grievances, to get it all out on paper. But don't stop there. Pray "God, because You willingly forgive all my sins, I choose to forgive my sister/brother. I forgive her/him for (say the list of things). I release them from my bitterness. Please cleanse and heal my heart and help us love each other the way You love us."

If you enjoy close family relationships, cherish them and remind them of your love today. Don't wait for tomorrow. And talk about the eternal perspective together. Do you and your siblings have assurance you'll enjoy heaven together forever? If not, what's holding you back?

Love for Learning

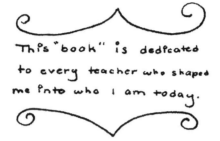

This "book" is dedicated to every teacher who shaped me into who I am today.

If you were around in the early 2000s, you may remember the popularity of "Baby Einstein" videos. Classical music played while colorful images of toys and puppets mesmerized the little viewers. Kayla absorbed them. That girl's brain was a sponge!

Most people get to enjoy car rides with babies and youngsters because they fall asleep—not Miss Kayla. She was always looking around—super aware! I remember her grandma telling me about their excursion to a grocery store. Kayla pointed to the sign "Quality Meats" and said, "Q!" This wasn't a surprise to me because I knew she could recognize letters and numbers, but I was surprised at how astonished Micky was. I was the last born in my family, so I wasn't familiar with young toddler development. I didn't know it was unusual. Don't all eighteen-month-olds know these things?

At two years of age, Kayla plowed through preschool workbooks with me during Rachel's nap times. Again, I thought it was normal and fun. Most toddlers think this is a blast, right?

I wrote to her when she was three: "Today was your first day of preschool. You've been excited about it since we signed you up six months ago! You had a great time! You came back with sidewalk chalk all over yourself." Kayla always enjoyed getting messy, especially if it had to do with art. Anyone who saw her splotched Darth Vader sweatshirt from painting drama club sets can attest to this.

When Kayla was eight, she took a test that qualified her as gifted. This explained her aptitude for learning. When we found out, we continued to dedicate her life, her gifts, and her talents to the Lord for His glory. But just because someone has an innate knack for something doesn't mean he or she will pursue it. Kayla tried to develop both in areas of God-given strengths *and* in areas of weakness.

I should *actively* pursue the traits that I'm weak in. They won't just come to me.

Where Kayla was strong, she reminded herself to give God credit. Here are creatively written instructions to herself.

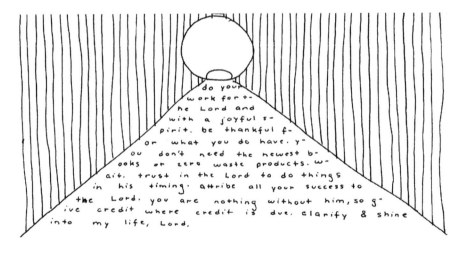

do your work for the Lord and with a joyful spirit. be thankful for what you do have. you don't need the newest books or zero waste products. wait. trust in the Lord to do things in his timing. attribe all your success to the Lord. you are nothing without him, so give credit where credit is due. clarify & shine into my life, Lord.

At age eleven, Kayla used a language learning app the library provided. This launched her fascination with languages—even Pirate! She included me in this. We had fun using our deepest voices and calling out phrases such as "ye filthy bilge rat!" to one another in jest.

In time, Spanish emerged as Kayla's favorite language. She was working on her fluency and accent because she wanted to live in Spain someday. But her fascination with languages (her "odd hobby" as she called it) extended to more than spoken languages.[8] She enjoyed learning sign language and even cryptic ones like shorthand and morse code.

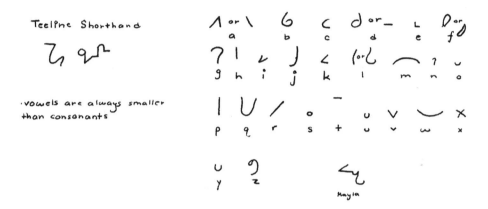

I take zero credit for her linguistic abilities. I barely got by with a C in French for the two required years in high school. Kayla received good grades, but she didn't strive for the sake of them or even reveal them to others. In fact, I came across her scores for the PSAT in a journal after she departed. She did not mention them even though she ranked high in the nation. I believe that even if she was not able to test well or get straight A's, Kayla would still have a love for learning.

---

[8] Kayla's love for language was featured in her last video, "My Odd Hobby":
bit.ly/KaylaLanguages

"It is certain that all persons of true genius have an invincible modesty & suspicion of themselves upon their first sending their thoughts into the world..." Jonathan Swift

In eighth grade, Kayla wrote a personal statement for the National Junior Honor Society. She concludes it with "I don't just learn for myself. I learn to teach others. I learn to make a difference. I learn to change the world."

Kayla was grateful for those who taught her. She prayed with thankfulness at the start of her final school year.

> Señor,
>
>   Thank you for the amazing school that I go to. Thank you for how much the teachers care about us and want to make a difference in the lives of their students. Please help me be a good witness to my teachers and friends this school year.

At the end of her last two school years, she and her best friend wrote notes to their teachers. She often wrote her teachers' and leaders' names as those she appreciated.

Mrs. Keller,

Thank you so much for the attention you gave me this year. I appreciate the time you took to enter my work into the photography competition (even if I don't make it in). You managed to make the class feel personal, even though I was squished in a back corner amongst a huge class. While I'm not taking photography next year, I'll continue practising what I learned this semester. Today (as I write this) I used the manual setting on my camera! I never thought I could use it before this class.

Kayla Durden

She typed the following two notes instead of handwriting them.

Mr. Zureick, You are a great chemistry (and homeroom) teacher. I love the independence you gave us but also the clear way you explained otherwise unconquerable chemistry ideas. I can't wait to be in AP Chemistry (and homeroom) next year.

Ms. Shuja, thank you so much for the effort you put into teaching your classes. I thoroughly enjoyed this year of English. It's hard to believe that I was most worried about this class at the beginning of this year. I just wanted to let you know that the pains you put into teaching us were not in vain. (I also really appreciated all the times you talked about Socrates) (Also, I'm determined to read Brave New World this summer.)

She was a blessing to her teachers, and they let her know it, too.

A True Wildcat

Querida Kayla,
    I just wanted to send a note to tell you I think you are awesome. Your passion & dedication for learning is inspiring. I love & appreciate how much you enjoy Spanish and the culture. You always work so hard at what you do, and I want you to know I notice. Thanks for all you do!
                    Sincerely, Sra Rudolph

After Kayla passed, the leader of Kayla's Academic Team had an "In Loving Memory" shirt made for the members to compete in that school year.

∞∞∞∞

Like Jesus, who "grew in wisdom and stature, and in favor with God and man" (Luke 2:52 NIV), Kayla modeled a hunger to learn and grow. I think of how young Jesus spent time among the teachers listening to them and asking questions. Kayla took every opportunity to learn. She often chose to listen in on conversations among adults not because she was nosy but because she wanted more understanding.

One of the hardest things for me to swallow when she passed was that all of her hard work and learning seemed to be wasted. She had no chance to attend college, find a career path, and serve the world with her knowledge. I was heartbroken at how it all seemed to be demolished without purpose or fulfillment.

But God was so gracious with me. He didn't let me suffer long with these thoughts. He put the right resources in front of me. I dove into learning about the biblical "new heavens and the new earth" to come. It helped to read Eldredge's *All Things New*. This book, along with the book of Revelation in the Bible, resolved my distress. NOTHING is wasted. Everything will be used. There is a sense in Scripture that we will continue to learn and excel forever. The Bible even talks about reigning with Christ in the age to come (Revelation 20:4-6, 2 Timothy 2:12).

Because of the way Kayla lived, I have a greater value of learning and growth in this life. I think she would invite us to be humble students, ever learning, growing, and seeking to honor God.

NOTHING YOU ever DO IS
USELESS
FOR THE LORD

Heart for Others

1 God & his
   family
2 my family
3 others

Kayla saved every note, letter, and card from loved ones. She even kept over eight hundred lunch notes that Jeff and I wrote to her. Her dresser drawers are full of memories: scrapbooks, childhood journals, pen pal letters, and programs from performances. She stored special items like a class t-shirt from second grade, her worn out, duct-taped color guard shoes, and even neatly folded wrapping paper from gifts she received. These things were treasured because of the *people* she associated with them. Her painting says it well.

Kayla wrote a prayer in eighth grade that expressed her desire to be a better friend.

Thank you for my good friends. Please guide me to be the best friend I can possibly be to them. I'm sorry that I'm not as good a friend as I should be. Help them to know that I do not want to be this way.

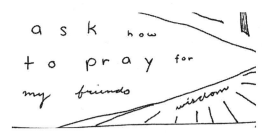

ask how
to pray for
my friends

Kayla was persistent in reaching out to her peers. She wanted them *all* to know Jesus, and she wanted them all to attend her youth group. She invited each one to LifeSpring's youth group until they yielded. This is because her church family was a genuine family to her. She wanted her friends to be a part of it. She recorded this desire when she was almost fourteen.

I want all my friends to go to heaven.

I share the good news because I want my friends to have the same joy I have.

Kayla prayed for and thought about where her friends stood with God. I am happy to say that she will see everyone on this chart in Heaven—they all gave their lives to Christ (names are blocked for privacy).

PEOPLE
I
WANT
TO
SEE
IN
HEAVEN

Datum / Date:

Here are some prayers about friendships in high school.

Thank you for the Christians in the group. Please help me to be a connector between different people. I want to be someone who facilitates new friendships. Also, please help me shine your light in my friendships. Please use me to bring people to you.

In Jesus' name,

amen

My God,

I can never stop thanking you for my incredible friends. I want what's best for all of them and I need you to do that. My friends come to me for advice, but I don't always have the right words to say. That's where I need you, Lord. I need your wisdom. I need your discernment, I need your words. Use me as your mouthpiece to say what you want me to say. And after I've spoken with them, move in their hearts and use every painful experience, every heartbroken moment to mold them into the person you want them to

As with most teenagers, friendships became the priority over relationships at home, but for Kayla, it took longer than was typical—until her sophomore year. Once on the friendship train, she sometimes needed to be refueled by God to continue loving us well.

Make every effort to be unified (in my family).

HEAVEN

WORLD

LOVE is the most important commandment.
The proof of God's LOVE is how we LOVE others.

Kayla cared deeply for her family members who didn't know Jesus like she did. Throughout her life, she prayed for them. While she was in children's ministry, she regularly wrote prayer requests for those loved ones. Angela Calabrese, her children's minister, saved each slip of paper and gave the stack to us when, normally, she would return them to the student upon graduation.

Much could be said about Kayla's heart for her extended family. But without giving a long speech, she *truly loved* her grandparents, aunts, uncles, and cousins. Most live at a distance, so she cherished holidays and vacations together. Some favorite memories include hiking and rafting, zip lining in an underground cave, gem mining in North Carolina, and celebrating Christmas in July more than once. She looked forward to being together, savored the time while there, and held onto the memories afterward. I am so grateful for the dear family that God surrounded her with while she was here.

Kayla respected our family heritage on both sides. When most preteens might not have been interested, she listened intently when her grandfather recounted family history in a lengthy conversation with her.

After I thought I found every last journal, I spotted two more on her bookshelf! These were a wonderful discovery—thankful journals. On each page she wrote ten things per day that she appreciated. Throughout her life, as she struggled with negative attitudes, my strategy was, "Tell me ten things you're thankful for." Most of the time, she'd roll her eyes, then look around the room and begin, "I'm thankful for walls, ceilings . . ." but by the end, she found things she was truly thankful for. It helped her snap out of negativity. I'm glad that she continued to see the value of choosing thankfulness.

She wrote each entry creatively (i.e. diagonally, upside down, with little figures by each item, and in categories like types of flowers, etc.). Her thankfulness extended past tangible elements, to include *all the people* in her life. There are names of friends, classmates, teachers, leaders, and family members. Often, she wrote a loved one's name, then listed ten qualities she was thankful for about them.

Her love for others includes her big heart for our pets: our sweet Shih Tzu, affectionate cats, and amusing chickens. Here is a video of her petting our tail-less cat one evening after folding laundry. The expression on her face is priceless.

 bit.ly/loveforcat

When he pawed at her window, she removed her screen to let him in, scooped him up, and buried her face in his outdoorsy smelling fur—even though she was slightly allergic.

Kayla also loved other people's animals. One year, she posted a picture of Tigre (Ashley's cat that she spelled in the British way) on her Instagram feed every day of his birthday month. I made a comment on one photo, "Has ever a friend loved another's cat so much?"

One day, Ashley inquired why Kayla always wanted a Golden Retriever since Kayla was usually unique in her preferences. From what I recall, these were her reasons:

1. Their loyal and tame temperament.
2. Their size. She always wanted to read while laying next to a big, safe dog.
3. Their fur color and their "mane" are lion-like. She wanted to have a relationship with a creature like Lucy has in the *Chronicles of Narnia*.

Now she is with her "Lion" along with her family members who have gone before, including my loving mother who went to Heaven when Kayla was only eleven months old.

I have many thoughts about her relationships in Heaven. Whenever I hear that another young believer has passed, I wonder if Kayla is now friends with that person. Perhaps she, along with C. S. Lewis, J. R. R. Tolkien, and Aslan himself, sit around having discussions in the most amazing book club ever! Who else might she be friends with? I can only imagine.

∞∞∞∞

Kayla's Grandma Duerler shared a concept that helps us endure—it's as if Kayla is in a distant land with no cell service, but we'll be together again and share stories of what we've been doing. She hasn't forgotten us and continues to love us from afar. If you knew her, even if you weren't close, you can bet that she loves you. If you didn't know her until now, you can be friends with her forevermore.

Deep Doodles

draw everything!

Kayla was eager to gain spiritual knowledge, understanding, and wisdom. She loved learning at church and was even a bit frustrated when she heard teaching she already knew, but she tried to receive something from every message.

I gave this note to her:

> Kayla, I appreciate how you take notes when listening to sermons. You never zone out, but you stay engaged. That reflects your reverence toward God and your respect for your spiritual leaders. Thank you for being this way.

She filled three journals over the last years as she listened to messages. Her friend liked them so much that Kayla gave her a completed journal, minus certain pages that she tore out for herself. After Kayla passed, Kendall was so thoughtful to return it to us.

Every weekend at LifeSpring, Kayla sat on my left. Every now and then I'd get a glance at what she was drawing. I knew better than to gaze too long, but what I saw were adorable, concise illustrations of the truths she wanted to remember. I even recall thinking "Those are amazing" followed by "but no one will ever see them." She posted a few on her personal Instagram page, but there were so many more. I felt they were meant to be shared. So with joy, I offer these to the world. I believe it honors her desire to reach people with God's good news, which is desperately needed these days. Since the day after she passed, we have been sharing these truth bombs via @she_had_no_regrets on Instagram and through posts at She Had No Regrets on Facebook.

Here are some of the full pages. Kayla also wrote her thoughts, opinions, and even physical feelings in little statements like "cold" or "tired." She also wrote silent suggestions or critiques, for example, about the video editing or the lighting. It highlighted her hunger for excellence in every area.

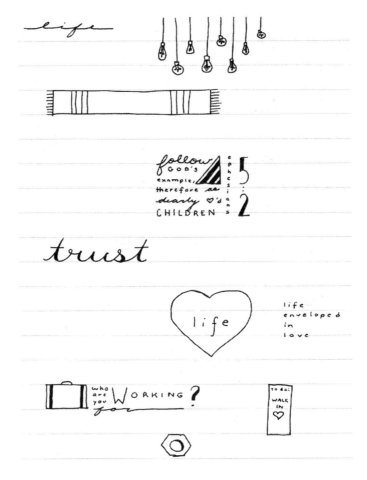

obediance is hard

Loving God means keeping his COMMANDMENTS & his commandments ███ ARE NOT burdensome

will-power

nothing will weigh you down more than disobeying God's commANDS

why should we obey God?

- he knows what's best for his kingdom
- he knows what's best for others
- he knows what's best for us

WILL I obey or REBEL

run, run, as fast as you can, you can't catch me, I'm a child of "the man ↑"

death ↑↑↑ sin

70 choices per day

what would happen if we obeyed & didn't have to think about it?

Whoever claims to live in him must live as Jesus did.

I will rise
on eagle's wings

if you died today,
where are you going & why

all the
EARTH
is mine

exodus 19

stargazing

nation

if you don't die tonight,
what are you going to do about tomorrow

jesus

you're

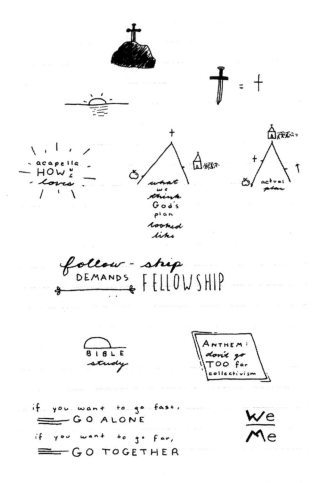

Almost a year after Kayla went to Heaven, some friends surprised us by printing many of the "deep doodles" we posted online and shallacking them onto a wooden picnic table they made. The table is located in a public space where many people can sit and contemplate.

∞∞∞∞

Not everyone is artistic with drawing, but everyone has a unique, God-given way of sharing truth and love. Just as Kayla developed her note-taking style from writings to drawings over time, you and I can develop our God-given gifts to help others grow and flourish.

Peacemaker

When Kayla was an infant, a thoughtful couple sent us an unusual baby gift. Instead of an item from a baby registry, we received a rustic piece of wall art that reads "Blessed are the Peacemakers." We believe God led them to give this prophetic gift. Kayla didn't just see it every day while growing up, she *became* its message.

Here is one of her first experiences being a peacemaker. It touches and breaks my heart at the same time. I wish I didn't have this experience to share, but it reveals her earliest attempts to create peace between people. She was not yet three years old.

> Tonight your Dad and I were having an intense conversation, and I spoke in harsh ways to him (which I'm not proud of). You witnessed the entire thing. You kept trying to change the subject by interjecting little phrases like "I gotta go potty" (when you really didn't), "Mommy, I love you," and "Let's play

I spy." Nothing stopped us until you folded your tiny hands, bowed your head, then looked up and said, "I'm pray that Mommy and Daddy get better."

When Kayla was seven, I wrote,

> You are mature in a lot of ways. You are learning to deal with conflict by saying things like "please stop that." You are also learning that people are not your enemy—Satan is, and he is lying to them. Right now, a girl is jealous of you, but you are understanding that she struggles with insecurity, and she needs Jesus. I'm so proud of you for having this perspective!

Kayla valued being at peace within herself. One of her phrases she often said in a calming, yet cute way was, "I'm . . . still . . . peaceful." She also wanted others to experience the peace she had. Many times she calmed me down when I was worried. Her logical mind helped me sort through what I was fixating over, and she reminded me to pray and trust God.

Eleven-year-old Kayla demonstrated this tactic when she was in a spelling bee. Jeff and I sat in the audience observing her behavior. Every few minutes throughout the long event, she closed her eyes to pray and calm herself.

As she grew in her social skills, she was sensitive to what caused breakdowns in relationships. Because of this, she prayed for a hurting friend in junior high.

> Please help   . She succumbs to the spirit of jealousy all the time. Guide her in repenting. She is losing friendships because of it.

When there was a fallout between two of her friends in high school, she tried to make peace between them. Kayla gently but firmly confronted them and told them they needed to talk it through. She set up a meeting time and place. According to her view on the matter, it was time for them to work it out.

After listening to a message on spiritual warfare, she wrote this paragraph. Oh, how everyone needs to understand this important truth.

I learned a lot! . . . about the armor of God and our weapons. We are battling a very real enemy. We are a people of power, and we are called to fight. We are not called to fight people. If we are fighting people, the battle is too small. We need to fight the enemy and his forces.

Kayla sometimes caused friction. She was never one to hide the truth, but sometimes she didn't use the best tact in her honesty. When Gabby had highlights put in her hair, Kayla didn't like the way the cooler shade looked with Gabby's beautiful warm skin tone. Kayla had strong opinions about color hues! She told her bluntly, but Gabby received an apology letter in the mail not long after.

Kaelie also shared a time that Kayla apologized to her. She couldn't remember what Kayla did wrong, but she was impressed because most people don't humble themselves and ask for forgiveness.

There were times Kayla never apologized to the person, but she prayed about her shortcomings. One April day in eighth grade, she wrote, "I'm sorry for being rude to Gabby, Emma, Ashley, Antonio, Chris, and anyone else I offended. Please help me be kinder and sweeter." Close to that time, she asked, "Please give me compassion for others. I need to be a better friend. Give me love. The never stopping, never giving up, unbreaking, always, and forever love. Please forgive me for being rude."

She wanted to be free from root issues that cause strife.

1. materialism (get rid of it)   ***Jesus*** FREAK
2. competition   ***Jesus***
                                              FREAK
3. jealousy
4. drama
5. gossip
6. anger   righteous indignation vs. anger
7. violence   not a problem-solver
8. fear of man
9.
10. laziness   ↓   take a sabbath

In another entry, she instructed herself.

Be humble

Be gentle

Be patient

Be peaceful

Try as hard as you can to create unity

She understood that God's ways of making peace are different than our ways.

Kingdom of God - wherever and whenever god is on the move

Dethrone pride and crown ~~of~~ love

The Kingdom is counter-cultural.

It's called the Upside-Down Kingdom.

I need satisfying water.

Read the Sermon on the Mount - Matthew 5

Humility - something I need

We mourn over the evil in the world and in us.

Meek not weak.

Turn the other cheek to ████

Seek to treat people right.

Buy good honey for food pantry.

Mercy

Motives matter.

Make peace with your enemies. Be proactive

Kayla kept this special note from Kelsey.

Kayla,

I know words of affirmation are not your love language 😊, but I wanted to take a minute to thank you for giving your Saturday mornings up to grow deeper in your faith with these girls. I have been so impressed by your maturity, Kayla. Watching you share your heart & thoughts with such honesty, grace, & boldness has been such a joy to watch. The way you have spoken up when you disagree has been so gentle and I know that can be so hard to do. THANK YOU for your willingness to share your time & heart with us. I'm looking forward to growing deeper! 😊

— Kelsey Herrick

The January after Kayla passed, the winter guard performed to a custom song. Krissy, the coach, reached out for quotes by Kayla. She came up with a beautiful performance about peacemaking, connection, and unity. Each of the girls who performed read one quote that was integrated into the soundtrack. It told a story of reaching out and befriending others who are different from one another. Half of the girls wore yellow, and half wore orange. In the beginning they were split into sides, and by the end they integrated as a whole to the tune of Amazing Grace.

In the final weeks of her life, Kayla was burdened over a friend's lifestyle choices. Kayla cared so much but dealt with it the wrong way. She didn't know how to fix it, so she took it to the Lord in prayer.

Almighty, Powerful, Wise God,

I still need your help. I don't have the wisdom on my own to know how to deal with this situation. I need your guidance. I think I know what you are trying to teach me though: humility; forgiveness; & sacrifice of stubbornness & personal image. I'll try to focus on those aspects of my heart.

In your beautiful son's name,

amen.

1 Thessalonians 4: 7
For God did not call us to be impure, but to live a holy life.

During this time, Marie (my dear friend whom Kayla is partially named after) texted me out of the blue. She told me she woke up that morning and heard "Pray for Kayla." She knew God meant Kayla Duerler. Overall, Kayla was doing great. Nothing major was wrong, so at first I wasn't sure what to tell her, but then this tense situation came to mind. I didn't know the details, I just knew there was some issue at hand, so Marie prayed for a resolution. Within a day, Kayla humbled herself! I believe that God wanted this conflict cleared up before Kayla departed, and He knew she needed support. He activated my friend, who herself is a peacemaker, to intercede on Kayla's behalf.

This was the day she wrote "apologize" as a to-do item. On a sticky note, she wrote the apologies and sent her friend the same message as a text. The conflict was bothering her not only for the behavior of the others involved but for *her own* failures.

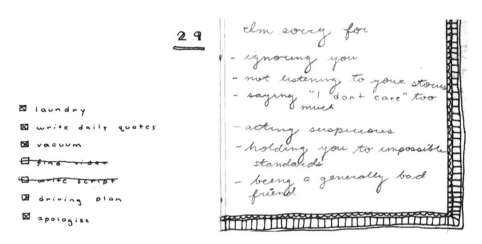

Then she wrote Psalm 28:7—her psalm of praise for the help God gave her. At this point she began committing this passage to memory as she had one more person to forgive in this scenario. Later, after she passed, I found where she sought to follow the instructions of Jesus when she was receiving unkind treatment from this young man: "Turn the other cheek to _____." She even included his name in one of her thankful pages. That very day Kayla stopped giving him death stares and began tolerating him even though he continued his behavior.

forgiveness

God of the heavens,

Thank you for the resolution that came out of this fight w/ ███████. Thank you for teaching me humility — as hard as it was.

in Jesus' Name,

Amen

PSALM 28:7

The Lord is my strength and my shield; my heart trusts in him, and he helps me;

My heart leaps for joy, and with my song I praise him.

Once Kayla fully forgave him, she had tremendous relief. Humbling herself wasn't easy, but it is God's way, and she trusted that His way is the best way. Her humility extended to telling me just three days before she passed, "Now I understand why I had a stye in my eye. I was judging _____ and _____." It took courage for her to admit being wrong, but it also brought freedom.

That day, I saw a lightheartedness in her that I hadn't seen since her birthday a month before. She was playful, cheerful, and delightful to be around. Months later, that friend surrendered her life to Jesus and told me that she wished she had done so when Kayla was still here. On Kayla's final night, she had a conversation with Ashley. Earlier that day, the guy was still saying things that should have caused Kayla to get upset, but Ashley was surprised by how peaceful and forgiving Kayla was toward him. The matter was truly settled in her heart. Kayla was ready to go without regrets.

> *Dear Lord,*
>
> *Thank you for revealing to me why I had a stye in my eye. I repent of the way that I treated him & please help me do better. On a separate note, please give me courage as I begin driving again and please help me stick to my plan. I'd love to be a blessing to my parents with my ability to drive.*
>
> *In Jesus' Name, Amen*

It's painful for Jeff and me to read the last lines of her last prayer for obvious reasons. She was pushing herself to learn how to drive—for *our* sake. I plan to share in my next book about how I dealt with my regrets, but, thankfully, we have assurance from Jeff's parents that Kayla was having a joyful, peaceful drive. She wasn't afraid and was proud of herself for how well she was doing. She came skipping back to the car after a restroom stop. They shared that even after the impact, she had peace till the end. She gave no cry or moan and her last breath was a quiet sigh. God was her strength, and He shielded her soul. Her heart trusted Him, and He helped her. Her heart leaps for joy, and with her song she praises him for all eternity.

She is . . . still . . . peaceful.

∞∞∞∞∞

God's timing is perfect. This morning Jeff and I had a strained conversation. I opened Kayla's journal from when she was only twelve years old. The Holy Spirit used her voice once again to make peace between us.

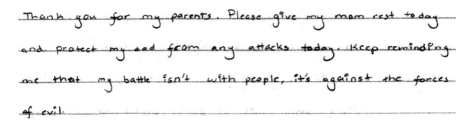

Thank you for my parents. Please give my mom rest today and protect my dad from any attacks today. Keep reminding me that my battle isn't with people, it's against the forces of evil.

Blessed are the peacemakers,
for they will be called children of God.
Matthew 5:9 NIV

Inside Her Prayer Life

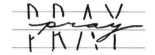

By now you've seen how Kayla prayed about practically everything. This chapter will focus on how her prayer life developed over time, and what we can glean from it.

When she was only two, I wrote:

> Tonight, Daddy and I were putting you to bed by singing songs and praying. Then you volunteered to pray for us. You put your little hands on our heads and prayed the way we do. First you thanked God for us. Then you said so quietly that we couldn't quite make it out, 'Please help . . .' I don't think you knew *what* to pray, but you knew *to* pray. It was so sweet that you wanted to bless us like we bless you.

Around the time Kayla went to junior high, her primary mode of talking to her Heavenly Father changed to praying on paper. Her prayers were conversational. She expressed her thankfulness and dependence on God, asked questions, confessed her shortcomings, fought spiritual warfare, and asked Him to work in people's lives.

The way she addressed Him is varied also. In junior high, she used "Dear Lord" most of the time, but also, "Dear God," "Dear Father," "Master," "Maker," and even "Maestro."

The following three prayers are from eighth grade.

3/3/16

Dear Lord,

    Thank you for the creativity you have given my family. Please help and guide us to use it for you. Thank you for creating beauty out of chaos, life out of death, and hope out of devastation. Thank you for creating sound. The scraping of pen against paper, "God is on the Move" on the radio, even my own breathing. Thank you for heat and cold. Please stop me from complaining about my life. It is good. I also need help with time management. I can't seem to get it right. Give me compassion for others like I've never had before. Please help me learn from _____, Help her realize that compassion is her spiritual gift. Do I need to tell her? Please help me to roll with the punches of life. I'm sorry for not being pure. Purify me, cleanse me of any bad things, search my soul, I want to be like you. Please give Daddy peace today. Please give me a Mary heart in a Martha world, and help me represent you. I need protection in the battle, give me the armor of God. Your will be done,

    In Jesus' Name,

    Amen

I believe the third sentence of that prayer was prophetic. She thanked Him for creating beauty out of chaos, life out of death, and hope out of devastation. There was nothing going on in her life that she should mention such themes.

While reading *Having a Mary Heart in a Martha World*, Kayla expressed how she wanted to be like Mary in the Bible who sat at Jesus' feet and listened to him instead of being like Martha who was too busy getting things done to spend time with Him. She wanted to stay in regular communication with her Father, so she wrote a reminder: "Bring journal to school and talk to God during the day."

2-28-16

Dear Lord,

It has been a long time since I used this journal. I'm sorry for my martha heart. Please let the Holy Spirit work in my soul so that I have a desire to be with you. Also, please draw ▮▮▮▮ close to you and comfort her while she is being called names. Give ▮▮▮▮ and me wisdom and discernment to know what to say. Clothe us with the belt of truth, the breastplate of righteousness, the shoes of the gospel, the shield of faith, the helmet of salvation, and the sword of the Spirit to fight the enemy. For we go out into a warzone every day and what good is fighting when we have no protection? Please give the Christians at school a love that compares to no other. An unconditional love that hits people hard. Please help us to be witnesses for you. I thank you for the sheer amount of Christians in my school. Please help us to live on mission and look for ways we can bring people to Christ. Thank you for restoring a bit of my Mary heart and help the seed you planted to blossum into a beautiful flower.

In Jesus' Name,

Amen

Here is a prayer of pure praise.

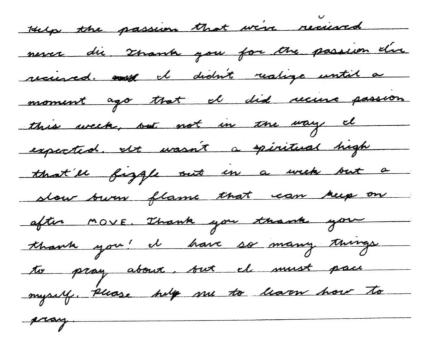

> Dear Lord,
>
> I praise you because you are a God of love. You are a God of mercy and justice. You are a God of creativity and laughter.
>
> In Jesus' Name,
>
> Amen

During her last summer, she returned from the MOVE conference and started a new prayer journal. She wrote twenty-three personal prayers in a little over a month. In her first entry, she was overflowing with thankfulness and spoke to Him about her realization.

Help the passion that we've received never die. Thank you for the passion I've received. I didn't realize until a moment ago that I did receive passion this week, but not in the way I expected. It wasn't a spiritual high that'll fizzle out in a week but a slow burn flame that can keep on after MOVE. Thank you thank you thank you! I have so many things to pray about, but I must pace myself. Please help me to learn how to pray.

She recognized her shortcomings but also God's renewal, and she was aware that she wasn't invincible.

> *Señor,*
>
> *Thank you for making me new every day. Thank you for helping me see how self-centered I am. Please help me change. Give me your eyes to see & your ears to hear. Shift my mindset, oh God, towards your kingdom. Give me drive to do kingdom work & let people see you through me. Don't ever let me forget how frail and small I am. Please teach me to pray.*
>
> *In Jesus' name,*
>
> *amen*

She spoke to the Lord about issues going on around her, but she also cared about the larger world.

> Querido Señor, Thank you for electricity and running water and air conditioning and my own room. I am blessed beyond all belief. I pray for those in Haiti who don't have these luxuries. Lord, transform Haiti . . . to a flourishing, vibrant, Jesus-worshipping country . . . "

At this point in her life, Kayla addressed God as "Señor," "Almighty God," "Abba" ("Daddy" in Hebrew), "My God," and the less formal "Hey God." In her last written prayers, she addressed Him as "Almighty, Powerful, Wise God" and "God of the Heavens." She only used these titles once in all of her writings. She was so close to meeting Him *in* the Heavens.

Early one morning after Kayla passed, Mr. Sams, a leader of Fellowship of Christian Athletes at the high school, gave a journal to each student and encouraged them to write their prayers because this practice made such an impact in Kayla's life. That afternoon, another teacher told me how glad she was to see an FCA member writing prayer requests in his journal. His first page was already full before the school day started!

Similarly, friends of ours who lead a youth group in northern Ohio told their students about Kayla's relationship with God. Every week they started their meeting by putting a scripture on the screen and allowing time for the students to meditate on it and respond to it. They were pleased that even the squirrelly junior high boys wrote in their journals. Everyone needs quiet moments of connecting with their Heavenly Father.

Many people, including children, have found Kayla's sincere prayer life inspiring. She honored and respected God, but also treated Him as her Friend and Father. It's so beautiful when she bursts out with praise. No doubt, she is doing that right now. Let's join her in having honest, personal, and reverent communication with the Lord.

There is no single, right way to pray. In fact, the Bible says, "We do not know what we ought to pray for, but the Spirit himself intercedes for us . . . in accordance with the will of God" (Romans 8:26-27 NIV). This definitely takes the pressure off. We don't have to do it perfectly. Also, the Bible tells us to use different kinds of prayers, like Kayla did.

> Pray in the Spirit on all occasions with all kinds of prayers and requests. Ephesians 6:18 NIV

Dear Father, help us to know You personally and have an ongoing conversation with You. Teach us to pray.

Passion for the Arts

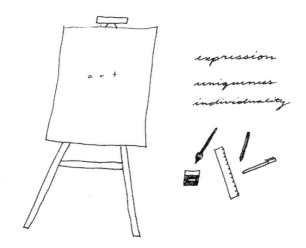

Her tiny, seventeen-month-old hand held a marker as she sat on my lap. I placed a piece of paper on my desk. She made a mark. Delight filled her little face! I handed her the next color, and she drew another line. As I gave her one new implement at a time, she was creating her first work of art. She kept making deliberate strokes until she used every marker. Fascinated with how the colors appeared under her command, she was hooked. That little hand was destined to create more than we could know.

When Kayla was a young preschooler, I remember observing her fine motor control as she carefully drew a spiral with a dot in the center. Upon showing her how to draw a basic face, she drew one then surprised me by adding eyebrows and hair! Soon to follow were family "portraits" and animal drawings. Her skills increased, and the developments were exciting to watch.

When Kayla was four, I asked her, "Kayla, do you love Jesus?" Her answer was, "Yes! When I get to Heaven, I'm going to give Him lots of hugs!" Then she asked me, "Mommy, do you think there will be paper and crayons and markers in Heaven so I can draw Him a picture?"

I wrote in her journal when she was nine:

> Yesterday we went to the conservatory in Columbus, Ohio. We enjoyed seeing the beautiful plants, the release of butterflies, a glassblowing demonstration, and many pieces of Chihuly's glass work. In the gift shop, you were determined to purchase a piece, and we supported your decision even though they were overpriced. You spent your own money on a unique glass lantern.

Kayla was so fascinated with glass blowing that I signed her up for a personal class. She was the youngest student the instructor ever worked with, and he was impressed with her maturity.

Around the age of ten, she learned to knit. Then sewing was a new fascination at twelve. She came up with the idea to slim down her school t-shirts by inserting a coordinating fabric in a strip along the sides. You can see a little of it in this pic of her among the flowers.

She and her Grandma did many sewing projects over the years, but the most meaningful was their last one—her kimono. They finished it right before her sixteenth birthday and she delighted to wear it in NYC. After she went to Heaven, her grandma took the extra fabric and made hair scrunchies out of it for all of Kayla's friends.

When Kayla was fourteen, she applied for Artworks, an apprenticeship program in which students paint impressive murals on buildings. Although Kayla put a lot of effort into her application and interview, she was not selected. Going through the process was a learning experience. In the end, I'm proud of how she handled not being chosen, and I'm relieved that she did not spend her summer days in downtown Cincinnati without us.

When Kayla was fifteen, we bought her a used Canon camera. A week later, she took three of her four photos that she entered into a statewide exhibit that took place after she passed. The cover of this book is one of them. She used that tiny detailed flower to represent herself on social media. You can see her photos here:

bit.ly/ArtShowKayla

Kayla also loved the arts in the music and rhythm sense. She began playing the flute in elementary school, then added the piccolo in eighth grade.

Kayla never took dance classes, yet spinning flags and other pieces of equipment for color guard came naturally. To watch her perform was a pleasure. One lady who attended football games said she enjoyed watching the halftime show and kept her eyes glued on Kayla because she was elegant, like a ballerina.

Kayla felt a strong attachment to her rifle and saber and affectionately called them "Christine" and "Erik" from *The Phantom of the Opera*. Here is her tryout video just a few weeks before she passed. She is on the right.

bit.ly/sabretryout

Speaking of musicals and Broadway shows, Kayla memorized every line of her favorites and never grew tired of them.

As a member of the high school Drama Crew, she painted sets. To prepare for *The Music Man*, she volunteered to paint the bookshelves for the library props. This was the perfect melding of her interests. I remember her excitement when she showed me her contribution to the show. Because of her hard work behind the scenes, the Drama Boosters created a scholarship in her name that is given every year to a dedicated member of the crew.

During her sophomore year, she became involved in a new art club at school. She painted a chair in the style of Van Gogh's *Cafe Terrace at Night*. Not only did it look like it, but she was able to paint it in sections with missing areas. She could have chosen the easy route of painting on the solid seat, but she challenged herself. Kayla and the other members of the art club donated their chairs for an auction to make money for the club. I regret not buying her work of art, but the family who bought the chair generously gave it to us.

The club was unnamed at the time of Kayla's involvement, but after her passing, Mrs. Cummings gave it the name Skye Studio. The club has gone above and beyond in honoring Kayla. For example, they held a month long art show in our local coffee shop. They collected hundreds of brown tags with notes about Kayla and strung them along the length of the main room. They also displayed custom art in her honor, including a gorgeous paper crane display.

One rainy day, Kayla placed a variety of paper samples outside so they would become crinkly. Combining two of her favorite things, rain and art, made her especially happy. Once the swatches dried, she sewed them onto the inner hardcover of a blank book to make her own artistic journal for her upcoming junior year.

In the spring, she gathered the daffodils in our yard and strung them throughout her room. Later, she did the same with weeds from the property where LifeSpring's new facility would be built. She dried the wild plants and gave them to her dad as a present, knowing how much that land meant to him and the church. He cherished such a thoughtful and unique gesture. We still have them on display.

We invited Kayla's friends to hang the flowers from her memorial because it is exactly what she would do. They adorn her room to this day, and I refresh them with any new flowers we receive.

Kayla was a methodical artist. In her last years, whenever she was about to embark on a new project, she made notes, practiced her handwriting, made sketches and storyboards, created paint swatches, and researched to make it the best version possible. I think the behind-the-scenes work is just as impressive as the finished product! She put such effort into achieving the final design. She also combined art forms. For example, she often took videos and photos of her process while making art. This added even more depth and layers to her experience.

In her last few years, she did the majority of her artwork in her room. Much of it I never saw until after she passed. It seems that she created because she enjoyed the process, not necessarily to show others.

A few weeks before her final day on Earth, she prayed, "Thank you for this artistic outpouring I've had recently." I believe God was compelling her to create, and to make her final journals incredibly detailed for us to have and cherish. She was leaving a piece of herself in her work.

Her last painting was made with one and a half days remaining. She painted with acrylics in her summer journal.

Although Kayla will no longer create new works of art here, I have been surprised to discover new-to-me pieces in various places that I had not seen before. For example, on the second to last page of her half-empty watercolor pad, I found this watercolor with ink sketches.

Here's what I notice: the heartbeat lines, the earthquake waves, the treasure, and the sun for a new day.

Not long ago, I discovered two graphic designs she saved on my computer. Just this week, I opened a book and found flattened ivy leaves that she picked from outside of her bedroom window. I'm hoping that I will continue to find more along the way, but even if I don't, I will see her create again.

Kayla's passing sparked my desire to create art again. After a hiatus for a few decades, I took up painting and drawing, and I am trying to focus on the process, not just the final results. I mainly draw birds, which Kayla loved.[9] For our second Christmas without her, I painted an elk buck for her dad. Using a mix of my watercolors and Kayla's watercolors, I worked in her room where she made so many of her pieces. I told Jeff it was from both of us because it is like something that she would have done for him. Ironically, when he opened it, Rachel saw it from across the room and asked if Kayla painted it. In a special way, I felt like she did because she inspired it.

---

[9] To visit my art site please visit: **bit.ly/JuliaKayArt**

Other people's creativity was ignited by her, too. So for the one-year anniversary of her going to Heaven, we hosted a Celebration of the Arts event. It was a powerful night when people displayed their God-given artistic talents to encourage one another. We also collected used instruments for the music program at the high school. The whole experience honored her life and was a blessing to the community. Jeff put together this special video that was shown at the event and now to incoming Skye Studio students.

 bit.ly/KDArtsSkyeStudio

∞∞∞∞∞∞

Kayla made an image of this verse. It describes the way she wanted to live.

> Make it your ambition to lead a quiet life: You should
> mind your own business and work with your hands . . .
> 1 Thessalonian 4:11 NIV

There was something about Kayla's hands. They were a focal point for her. Instead of taking selfies of her face, she both drew and took many pictures of her hands.

We don't fully understand her fascination with covering her hands with ashes a month before she departed. In fact, the photos she took have been upsetting for me to look at and hard to think about. Only just recently was I able to not quickly scroll past those sixteen photos on her phone. As I bravely peered closer, I saw that she took a picture of a beam of light crossing over her darkened hand. It looks like she wiped the ashes away where the beam was. Then she formed a peace sign with her fingers. I feel like the dots are connecting. I wonder if it was a prophetic act done exactly one month before her body was cremated. Not that she knew what was coming, but the Holy Spirit inside her did. And I'm finally feeling that those pictures aren't meant to torment me, but to demonstrate what the Bible says in Isaiah 61—that God makes beauty from ashes for those who mourn. He is bringing light through the darkness and giving us peace.

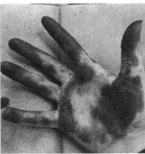

Now I'm thinking beyond my little world. I want God to do this for everyone who experiences loss and heartache.

Beauty from ashes. Only He can do such miraculous work.

What About Romance?

"I'm starting to get used to my friends talking about boys," Kayla mentioned to me as a preteen, though she wasn't interested in boys yet. I am thankful that she was slow to "awaken love" before the time was right. I prayed for her as she was growing up that she would be preserved from unnecessary heartbreaks and attachments. I believe God answered these prayers.

She was never a big romantic. When she had crushes, she kept them to herself. Because of that, I don't have a lot of information, but here are some clues in bits and pieces that I picked up.

Kayla wanted depth in her relationships. The following book review reveals her displeasure with shallow romances.

Words in Deep Blue

CATH CROWLEY

Contemporary. It was a contemporary. I can handle a fantasy romance, but not a contemporary romance. I honestly just stayed for the bookstore. Both main characters were whiny & immature, especially Henry. Yeah, Amy broke up w/ you, but you don't need to be pathetic. My favourite part was the letters in the Letter Library. This story wasn't character or plot based, it was setting based and not executed well, though that might be my perspective of contemporaries.

To my knowledge, only one young man asked Kayla out. I recall her telling me how bluntly she said, "No." I gently explained that kindness and respect are important even when turning someone down.

When she wrote her book review of *My Lady Jane*, she got excited about the slow development of a relationship. She exclaimed, "NO INSTA-LOVE! It was amazing! I fell for G with Jane."

Her "Fellowship of the King" Pinterest page includes an image with the message "Dear Future Husband, find God, find yourself, then come find me."

She posted this quote by C. S. Lewis: "A woman's heart should be so close to God that a man should have to chase Him to find her."

She also included a picture of a couple holding hands as they study their Bibles together with the caption "Relationship Goals."

We found some telltale signs from her last journals about where her heart was with this topic. When she became a teen, I encouraged her to make a list of qualities she wanted in a husband and to begin praying for the man who would fulfill them. This is what I did as a young woman, and God answered my prayers by handpicking Jeff for me! On June 3, Kayla had on her checklist of things to do: "future marido [husband] list." Then in another journal she jotted some ideas of what she wanted in a man.

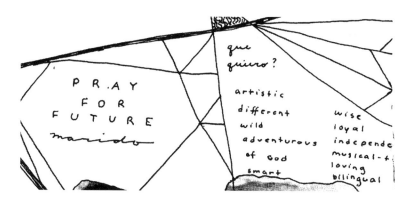

In another entry, written in Spanish and found among her notes during a youth conference, she made a confession. She did not want to notice boys so much because she didn't want anyone to come between her and God. I'm glad she wrote this. It assures me that she has exactly what she wants because her main desire was for Him, not for an earthly relationship.

In her last letter to herself, she said, "Keep dedicating your life to Christ, chicos are not important."

In her freshly started art book, I discovered the tiniest scraps of burnt paper amidst the mostly blank pages. She labels them, "getting over a crush." The date is exactly one month before the accident.

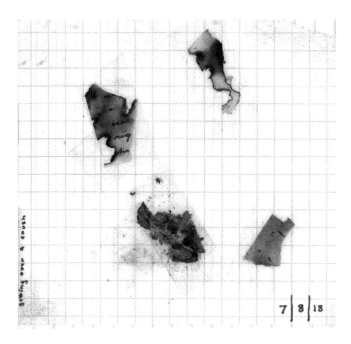

Oh, how hard it is to let go of a crush when you are sixteen! It looks like she burnt her own writing about him—one more preparation for the departure she didn't know was coming, like sealing the end of a cord with a flame. On that same day, she put this quote on her Instagram feed: "Do not go gentle into that good night . . . but rage, rage against the dying of the light. Dylan Thomas." Perhaps this act was her raging against the feelings and distraction that could take her passion away from her True Love.

Creative Writing

Kayla was not only an avid reader, but she tried her hand at authorship in a variety of styles. She drew a graphic novel in ink. Here is one page from *The Red Scarf*.

For a Spanish assignment, she wrote a fantasy book for children. She painted the illustrations in watercolor. I like how the character looks like Kayla.

ELLA AGARRA UNA VELA Y LA ENCIENDE. ENTONCES, ELLA ANDA DE PUNTILLAS SUBE LAS ESCALERAS. PASADO EL BLASÓN DE LA FAMILIA. PASADO LA PINTURA DEL MAR HASTA...

She grabs a candle and lights it. Then, she tiptoes upstairs. Past the family crest. Past the painting of the sea until...

Here are a few of her many pieces I have not shared on social media because her writing is too small, and it would be difficult to read. These are responses to writing prompts from her ninth grade advanced English class.

The following stream-of-consciousness response is interesting because she completely avoided talking about goals for high school, something she would normally be eager to discuss. Perhaps it was not a coincidence that her mind went blank when trying to foresee the next four years.

9 36/36 Verygood!

What do you hope to accomplish in the next four years?
Tick, tick, tick the hands of the
classroom clock taunt me as I struggle
to come up with an idea. What do I
want to accomplish in four years? My
brain wonders and I consider running
out of the classroom but I dismiss the
idea. How can I get out of doing this
dreadful prompt? I can't use song lyrics,
so Hamilton is out of the picture. Maybe
if I write sloppy enough, Mr. C won't be
able to grade it and I can have more time
to finish. No, he will just give me a 0.
I need to think, what goals do I have
for high school? I could write about getting
good grades, but everyone will do that. Oh
no, my pulse is speeding up, I'm getting
light-headed, and my brain is turning to
cotton candy! A glance around the room
reveals that the other kids are still writing
but are almost finished. I was in Power
of the Pen, why can't I come up with one
measly idea? I wipe my sweaty palms on
my pants and look around the room again.
I am the only one not finished. My vision
begins to go fuzzy and I panick. Just as
I am about to black out, I hear the sweet
relief of the bell. As I am leaving the
classroom I cannot help but grin - I had
beaten the prompt!

This science fiction piece deals with a unique perspective on dying.

"Papa, no!" a girl sobs. Her teary eyes expose her anguish and though I do not know why she is upset, I feel a need to comfort her. As she continues crying, I glance around at the unfamiliar surroundings, trying to figure out where I am. The dimly lit room is furnished with some careworn furniture and is lined with bookshelves bursting at the seams. My attention is drawn to the girl who has stopped crying. "Do you really not know who I am?" she chokes out. "No" I reply. "I am your daughter." "Mina, is he ready?" a tall man enters the room. The girl, Mina, nods mutely. The man strides over to my chair and wheels me to an adjoining room. A handful of people are huddled around a table. Mina walks around the table a puts her head on the shoulder of a dark-haired man. The tall man stands to my left and produces a piece of paper. He breaks the spell of silence like a pebble dropped in a pond. "We are gathered here today to read and honor the last wish of Viktor Borchert. 'My dear family, I have been diagnosed with a debilitating disease (as you know), and I am slowly losing my memory. Your Mutter passed away some time ago and now I must follow. The day I forget the name of my dear daughter Mina—" here the girl begins crying again "is the day I wish to depart from this life.'" The tall man folds up the paper and places it on the table. "Viktor goes on to describe how the procedure is to be done." The tall man opens a briefcase and ~~xxxxxxxxxxxxxxxxxxxxxx~~ I watch in fascination as he draws out a gleaming needle. "The method is by shot which I will insert into his upper forearm. I can promise you, it will not be painful." He approaches me and as the needle nears my skin, I look up and lock eyes with the crying girl. The last thing I see is her eyes, full with a fusion of love and grief before everything is black.

You may find Kayla's treatment of death a little matter-of-fact here. Interestingly, she conveyed a similar sentiment in her *final* academic piece. We found it on the last page of schoolwork in her sophomore year binder. It was an ethics exercise where students explain their response to whether Heinz should have broken into the laboratory to steal a drug to save his wife's life.

the HEINZ dilemma

Should Heinz steal the drug?
No, stealing is wrong no matter which light you put it in. I know, the druggist is "stealing" the man's money, but what he was doing isn't illegal. Buddy, just let your wife die. If it's her time to go, then it's her time to go. You also don't know if it'll work, it may make her feel more pain. I know it breaks your heart, but time's up, alea iacta est.

Notice the last line "alea iacta est" (the die is cast)—this time she clearly associated it with *time being up*.

∞∞∞∞∞

We find it immensely helpful that Kayla did not live with a fearful or foreboding outlook on death. It did not spark terror, alarm, or even trepidation in her. In fact, it was the opposite. Her faith in Jesus' promises made her anticipate when her time would come.

We now imagine *her* coaching *us* in how to handle the feelings we associate with mortality. I don't think she would want us to shut down our emotions. However, she wouldn't want us to be their helpless victims either. She would want us to remember God's promises about life after this life. She would want us to remember that He is sovereignly working to restore what's broken and to make all things new. And that those who turn to Jesus can live without being afraid of the end of this earthly existence.

> Because God's children are human beings—made of flesh and blood—the Son also became flesh and blood. For only as a human being could he die, and only by dying could he break the power of the devil, who had the power of death. Only in this way could he set free all who have lived their lives as slaves to the fear of dying. Hebrews 2:14-15 NLT

Becoming a Leader

He is how a quiet girl became an up-front leader. Starting in elementary school at age ten, her teachers recognized her integrity and chose Kayla to be on a student leadership team. During that same time, she helped lead the LifeSpring kids' worship time with choreographed motions rather than singing. She mouthed the words because she thought she didn't have a good voice, but she was effective at leading with movement.

Then, before she went to junior high, I launched the Club 56 Leadership Team for fifth and sixth graders. I was excited to lead her and the other students farther along in their faith. Some of the topics we studied included having "Godfidence" (a confidence that comes from God) and having a heart to love others.

She invited a long-time friend to become a member. That was an important step because, in time, Kennedy chose to follow Christ and be baptized. This was an answer to a prayer Kayla had been voicing since first grade. Kennedy will see her again!

Next, Kayla entered our church's youth ministry. In ninth grade, she was a member of the student leadership team. Her leader, Ed Hampton, shared that she always sat in the same spot at the head of the table. She brought her journal and had clearly spent time with the Lord that week, and she took notes on what they talked about in the meetings. When he asked her to read from the Word, she usually read from her Spanish Bible and translated on the fly which made him smile.

Another adult leader, Meghan, shared this memory with me.

> I didn't get to be with Kayla too long in youth group, but one of my favorite experiences with Kayla, and, oddly enough, my very first interaction with her, was when we loaded up in cars to go downtown to pray for and feed the homeless. I had my car full of girls, and Kayla was one of them. We got into a conversation on books and movies and when one particular series came up, Kayla talked about not reading them even though all the other girls LOVED them and raved about them. She said, "My mom doesn't want me to." I asked her, "How do you feel about that? Do you think you might read them when you get older?" She responded SO confidently, "I respect that my mom doesn't want me to read them, and I plan to honor that." All I could think to myself is, *Oh my gosh, who is this girl!?* It was the first conversation I ever had with Kayla, and I just love the way she modeled honoring her parents to her friends. It showed me a lot about her right off the bat. Kayla was never going to give into peer pressure.

Mrs. Haas told about Kayla's boldness to stand for what she believed in. She said,

> Everybody knew Kayla had a faith. She didn't beat people over the head with the Bible, but she lived what she believed. If somebody said something contradictory to her faith or her values, she would say, "That's not the truth" and when they came back at her, she'd say, "You're wrong" and give them a sad look like, "You really don't get it."

She also shared, "Kayla was a strong part of our junior high Bible study that we had on Friday mornings, but she wasn't a person up front. Kayla was very content to stay in the back. She wasn't somebody out for show." That's true. Yet, despite her tendency to not place herself in front, the Holy Spirit compelled her to step before her peers one of those mornings to share evidence that God is their Creator. In order to graciously counteract macroevolution, she planned her defense and equipped her peers with an explanation and activity. She saved her presentation on my computer. Interestingly, her great grandfather gave a convincing argument against atheistic evolution when he was a med student at Case Western Reserve generations before.

Today I'm going to talk about how God is the awesome designer of all creation. I'm going to read Isaiah 45:18 (reading...). This means that God formed us intentionally. It wasn't just an accident.

I'm going to show a video clip that shows the chances of life forming on its own.

It is from a documentary called Expelled (Show the cover). It's about educators and scientists who are being ridiculed and fired for merely believing that there might be evidence of "design" in nature. (play video 1:57 min.)

Now you can see the chances for yourself. (Pass out books from the bookshelf) Everyone turn to page 22. Read the first word on the page and write it down. Then write every 5th word on the page until you have 15-20 words. I'm going to pass Expelled around while you're working. (....) Now read the sentence you just created. Did it make sense? The chances of life forming on its own are as good as creating a sentence that makes sense from random words.

This week I encourage you to show a friend that book activity and tell them about our awesome creator.

At the end of Kayla's eighth grade year, Mrs. Haas wrote to her.

As a fourteen-year-old, Kayla wrote: "I am a leader. To be a good leader, I need to be diligent— spontaneous, not cold and calculating—tender, not bossy."

In the marching band, Kayla chose color guard over an instrument. Her entrance into the guard world started a year after her best friend joined in seventh grade. Kayla wanted to enlist with her, but the winter competitions were on Sundays. She understood why we said no. Our family prioritizes church involvement. But the following year, LifeSpring established a Saturday evening service, so we allowed her to join winter guard because she wouldn't miss worshipping with her church family.

For the winter of their freshman year, Kayla and Ashley made detailed plans for an extra season of practice for the color guard crew. Though they were young and the program never materialized, the girls came up with thorough lesson plans and a checklist of what they wanted to cover. Leadership was in their veins.

The girls looked to Kayla to braid their hair, but they were required to put their hair back with a "bump" on top for performances. None of them liked the underneath teasing and top coating of hair spray, so Kayla took charge and created a petition for "The Removal of the Bump." It accrued a lot of signatures, but was ineffective to create change.

In high school, she and Ashley recruited more friends, and color guard became a major sphere of connection and influence. She loved dancing, spinning, and tossing, but she loved her comrades most of all. Kayla ended up spending more time with the marching band than with us during her last two fall seasons, but none of us would have had it any other way. Marching band was like another family for her.

Ironically, when Kayla was four years old, Jeff noticed her watching Baby Einstein's "Meet the Orchestra." He asked, "Kayla, would you like to be in a band someday?" She responded, "No, I wouldn't want to leave you guys!"

Bailey, who was a senior when Kayla was a freshman, started a tradition. As the girls were stretching their arms with their hand out, she ran around and gave each person a high five. When she graduated, she passed that role to Kayla. Then, after Kayla departed, the girls chose Kaitlyn to be the high-fiver. This is because each upperclassmen chose a freshman they looked out for and Kaitlyn was Kayla's freshman. It means so much that Bailey and Kaitlyn chose to be baptized at Kayla's memorial service (along with more than twenty others). They will see Kayla again, too.

As a sophomore, Kayla was the Dance Captain. Jeff and I recall watching her during the home football games. When the color guard was not performing, she was behind the stands where the marching band played pep songs. We stood many yards away, observing her conduct while chatting with friends. We noticed that she never rested. Instead, she helped the less-experienced girls improve their tosses. Encouraging and patient, she gently instructed them with a smile on her face. She would demonstrate a toss or movement and then have them try it. She did this repeatedly, without any sign of frustration. Later, when we talked to her about it, she told us she hoped to benefit the band overall by training the young ones to do their best.

Here is a video of Kayla leading their warm up. I cried when I watched it for the first time recently. The song could not have been more perfect for what was to come. Please start at 2:40.

 bit.ly/InMyHeartWarmUp

During the spring semester, Kayla decided to try out for Drum Major for her junior year. Here is part of her application:

My main leadership style is democratic. I always ask my teammates and those I'm leading before

I make a decision that will affect them. Therefore, I am not commanding, as others who don't ask before making decisions. I am an affiliate in the sense that I am a peacemaker. I try to break up fights, acting as the moderator as often as I can. I have learned to be a coach from color guard. I can't count the number of times I've said, "Try this." I spend quite a bit of time teaching the young guard girls how to do tosses or choreography. I'm not visionary because, though I have internal goals, I don't know how to communicate them to others. I also don't want to force my goals on other people. I believe that everyone I'm leading should have some chance for creativity.

The position of a drum major gave her the opportunity to be a positive influence. During this brief time, she was in the zone, eager to serve her fellow band members with all her heart and energy. The timing was just right. She was in that role for the intense weeks of summer band camp. Her dedication, joy, commitment, and hard work made an impact that continued long after she departed.

Today is the first day of preband camp & I'm super excited & kinda wary. Thank you that I'm not nervous. Thank you for placing me in this position & help me to make a difference in this band. I want to shine your light & passion to all the kids. Please give me energy & help this day to go smoothly.

25·6·18

Almighty God,

Thank you thank you thank you for putting me in the position of drum major! Thank you for Mr. Egan's dedication to the music program & his adaptability. Thank you for each of the directors & their willingness to spend time with ungrateful teenagers. Thank you for the kids who join marching band. Thank you for the band's improvement over the years to get us to this year. Thank you for the way your spirit will move this summer & rest of the year.

In Jesus' Name,
AMEN

to pray for—

relationships	creative team
passion	(cohesivity)
team bond	Holy Spirit move!
kindness	Jesus earthquake
directors	talent

Kayla's prayers were answered.

This is how Brian Egan, Kayla's band director, described Kayla at her memorial service:

> Kayla was our rockstar. She was our student who always showed up. You may not have noticed her right off the bat, but your eyes were drawn to her. She always performed. She gave 110% no matter what. Even if her knees were bothering her, even if she was tired, she went out there.

He shared that he had the privilege of knowing her for six years when she played flute in the front row, asking him every day when she could also play the piccolo. He explained,

> Kayla was the most curious kid I've ever met in my life, there was no fakeness about her . . . she was just Kayla from her faith to everything. She was amazing. Being around her was a joy. Kayla brought everybody together, not for her to be the center of attention, but to bring everybody in, to welcome everyone. And everybody knew Kayla was there to support them. She was an inspiration to all of us.

In this last photo taken the day before the accident, Kayla's strength and *Godfidence* are clear. Kayla's time on earth ended on a high note.

Band 2018

∞∞∞∞

The marching band and color guard dedicated every performance of that season to Kayla. They all wore a key necklace with her name imprinted on it and two brown beads. An "In Loving Memory" logo was incorporated into their uniforms. They brought along her saber that they wrapped in brown tape for every performance and competition. Ben Calabrese, who was like a brother to her since fourth grade, became a drum major their senior year. He continued the tradition by placing that saber on his stand as he conducted, then he brought it to the awards ceremony each time and placed it on the ground in front of their representatives.

In Loving Memory

K.D. 2002 - 2018

Other high school marching bands in the Cincinnati area did special tributes that first season as well. Kayla's dear friend from childhood, Jaylee, a drum major at Walnut Hills High School, led her band to dedicate a performance for Kayla and even had special t-shirts made. Their show was "Come Together." It fit perfectly with Kayla's ideals of unity.

The members of our marching band continued to sense Kayla's love for them. Throughout that first season without her physical presence, an unusual number of rainbows showed up at Friday night games and competitions. One time a rainbow appeared when it was completely sunny, and there were no clouds overhead. Rain began during the National Anthem, and the rainbow formed behind the stadium over the school building, where the band members could see it as they played. A teacher sent me pictures of the gentle phenomenon. Then there was a rainy evening that stands out from the rest. I close this chapter with a special band member's beautifully written explanation.

Kayla's Gift
By LiLi Russell

A fine mist gently moistened my hair and cheeks as I stepped onto the grassy practice field. The drizzle reminded me of a passionate chef sprinkling his signature dish with the perfect amount of seasoning. Everything about the evening felt right, even though the cool night air altered the sound of my instrument, making each note shriller.

We ran through our show several times before forming a tight circle and playing "You'll Never Walk Alone" to honor our newly departed drum major and friend, Kayla. The night's performance was dedicated to her memory. Tucking my trombone beneath my armpit, my shoulder ached as much as my heart.

Chatter soon filled the air, distracting me from the pain and calming my nerves as our dysfunctional band family began its lengthy march toward the competition arena. Feelings of pride and confidence grew with each precise step. As soon as our feet hit the puddle-dotted turf, an ethereal rainbow hovered over the stadium. I breathed deeply and knew I was part of something special. The baritone player next to me gave my thoughts a voice, whispering, "This is Kayla's gift."

The full-color sign was just what I needed, moving me to give all that I had. The sentiment was universal, and it showed in the strength of our performance. Then, as we finished playing and rushed off of the field, the beautiful rainbow faded away as if on cue.

We awaited our results, shedding tears and marveling over what we had experienced. A trophy suddenly seemed insignificant. Kayla was with us in spirit, and that was enough.

It's Like She Knew Somehow

"The impossible could not have happened, therefore the impossible must be possible in spite of appearances." —Hercule Poirot

Kayla loved a good mystery. She was on a huge Agatha Christie kick in her last months. Since her departure, we have discovered many clues that were dropped like bread crumbs on a trail to Heaven. I sometimes wonder if Kayla is watching us as we find the hints that God knew all along. She was probably unaware of all the foreshadowing in her life. But God knew.

Conversations with Kelsey

[Background to this conversation: LifeSpring grew to need a new facility. The church already owned land from many years before, and the time finally came to begin construction. This "Community Commons" would not only house our services and ministries but also an early learning center, an indoor playground, and a coffee shop. A year after Kayla passed, Kelsey relayed this conversation to us.]

When I was pulling into the groundbreaking yesterday, the Spirit brought back to my memory a moment I had with Kayla, and I was overcome with so many emotions. I believe this was prophetic and a message God wants me to tell you.

About a month before Kayla went to be with the Lord, Caleb and I were driving her home from our Saturday morning group, and we were at the stoplight by the library.

CALEB: Kayla, what are your thoughts on the new building and the TRANSFORM campaign?

KAYLA: I'm so excited for you guys.

KELSEY: What about you?

KAYLA: Well, I won't be here for it. But I'm so excited for all of you and the things that are going to happen in that building. I can't wait to see it all come together. I love the vision of the community center.

When she said she wouldn't be here for it, we assumed it was because of college and Spain, but now I see that God was moving ahead of us to give us that sweet and powerful moment with her.

In my next book, I will have a detailed chapter that explains the many types of premonitions and prophetic insights we received, but I want to share a few that come from her pen here.

During the MOVE conference, just months before the accident, Kayla wrote about "The Jesus Earthquake" of which she should be part of the epicenter. She said it will start with her home, then hit her school, then her community, and the shock waves should keep radiating.

I'll share some things I learned: the jesus earthquake— when we go home, we should be the epicenter of the jesus earthquake. we'll start with our home, then our school, then our community and the shock waves should keep radiating

She placed this 5x7 piece of paper on her computer desk as a reminder. It was the first thing I noticed when I went into her room after I heard about the accident—the accident which set in motion a series of impactful tremors that have produced great good in our home, the school, our community, and beyond.

EARTHQUAKE
epicenter

Another stunning discovery a few weeks later was this poem by Charles Dickens. She wrote it in her planner *literally* one year before her memorial service. It could not be stated more eloquently or accurately for what was to come.

> " I see a beautiful city
> and a brilliant people
> rising from this abyss.
> I see the lives for which
> I lay down my life
> peaceful
> useful, prosperous, and happy
> I see that I hold a sanctuary
> in their hearts
> and in the hearts
> of their descendents
> generations hence. "

We noticed something intriguing in Kayla's writings from her final days. Her sermon notes have this statement, "Glorify your daughter so your daughter may glorify you." Then she wrote the same thing in her prayer journal the next day, which was *precisely one month* before her passing. Kayla was personalizing Jesus' prayer from the very end of his earthly life right before *he* went to be with the Father:

> When Jesus had spoken these words, he lifted up his eyes to heaven, and said, "Father, the hour has come; glorify your Son that the Son may glorify you . . . I glorified you on earth, having accomplished the work that you gave me to do. And now, Father, glorify me in your own presence with the glory that I had with you before the world existed." John 17:1,4-5 NIV

8 · 7 · 18

Almighty God,

Yours is a name to be glorified. Every rock, tree, insect, and river declares your name holy. Let our praise echo your greatness. Your beauty is witnessed in the clap of thunder before a storm and in a child's laugh. Let our praise echo your greatness. You restore, renew, and rebuild this broken world. Demons flee at the sound of your name. Let our praises echo your greatness. Give the church insight into how to worship and glorify your daughter so that your daughter may glorify you.

Amen

In that prayer, she proclaimed what those who love and miss her are experiencing: "You restore, renew, and rebuild . . ."—such a wonderful declaration of truth!

Another intriguing discovery was that we found the missing piece of the above image glued into her daily planner. It was about an unusual experience she had the previous day where she felt her past, present, and future selves coalesce.

I had a cool experience today. After working on chemistry for a few hours I was tired, so I decided to listen to some music while lying on the picnic blanket & look at the sky. I listened to ~~Panic!~~ some of Panic! at The ~~Disco's~~ new album, "Pray for the Wicked." Anyway, as I listened I became super nostalgic and I began to feel like my past, present, and future selves all combined in a few ~~songs~~ time. (7·7·18)

The next two pages are covered in ashes. So her experience of taking those photos of her ash-covered hands happened the day after her prayer to glorify God and her "out-of-body" type experience, *all exactly one month before she passed.*

Then with only twelve days remaining, she wrote the word LOVE on her wrist and an X on her palm. To me, it seems like she was contemplating sacrificial love—how true love is laying down one's life for others, just as Jesus did for us. I believe Kayla was willing to die, if given a choice, so that others could live eternally.

Finally, just three days before her final moment here, Kayla wrote these two phrases on the last page of her sermon notes.

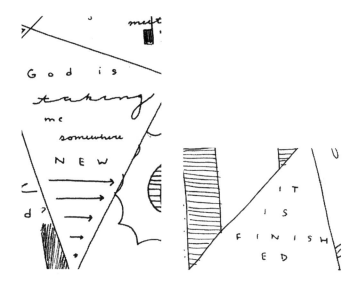

That evening, Jeff had a "random" conversation with her about death. He doesn't know why he asked, but he posed the question to Kayla and Rachel on the way home from youth group: "Do you ever think about dying?" The conversation dropped in the car, but she picked it back up when he was saying goodnight to her. Kayla told him that she wasn't afraid to die. She just wouldn't want her friends to be angry at God. She also mentioned something about wanting to write a will but not about what to do with her stuff. It was deeper than that. Weeks later we found her simple instructions to herself at the end of the chapter in *Crazy Love* about death. It simply states, "Write to Ash if I die." Ashley had not surrendered to Jesus yet, and it was a huge concern for Kayla. But on the very day of the accident, God gave Kayla the desire of her heart. Miraculously, Ashley was *not* angry with God and instead surrendered her life to Christ! They will get to enjoy all of eternity together forever.

Angela Calabrese, our dear friend who was Kayla's children's minister, said this at the memorial (and we wholeheartedly agree):

If Kayla could see Ashley truly surrender her life over to Christ. If she could see all of you sitting here hearing God's Word, Kayla wouldn't think twice about getting in that car again. I can see her rushing to that car and hopping in. And her response without any tears, without any sadness, would be "Christ did that for me on the cross."

∞∞∞∞∞

Hints. Clues. Signs, perhaps? We don't have any reason to believe Kayla thought her life on earth was nearing its end, but we look back with amazement at how it's *as if* she knew, somehow, that her time on earth was short. We wonder if God softly prompted Kayla to write and do certain things for *our* sake. Why? To show all of us that nothing gets past Him.

Trusting the Father's ability to work everything out—even what we tend to look at as premature death—helps us when we are hurting.

Perhaps you're wrestling with something that happened in your life. You don't understand why. Everything inside you is fighting against it being real, but it's impossible to change it. You can't rewind, and you may not understand, but you have an opportunity to accept things beyond your ability to understand and to trust God to bring good out of them.

> "For my thoughts are not your thoughts, neither are your ways my ways," declares the Lord. "As the heavens are higher than the earth, so are my ways higher than your ways and my thoughts than your thoughts." Isaiah 55:8-9 NIV

Her Eternal Perspective

do something eternal

Despite having great health, Kayla seemed to be constantly aware that life is short. Eternity was on her mind. She lived out Psalm 90:12: "Teach us to number our days, that we may gain a heart of wisdom" (Psalm 90:12 NIV).

Conversations with Kelsey

The last chapter we read and discussed is titled "Your Best Life . . . Later." We discussed this question in one of our very last groups at the end of July 2018.

KELSEY: Girls, Sometimes I hear about people getting in car accidents or getting cancer, and I think it could never happen to me. Do any of you think that?

KAYLA: No. I know I could die at any moment, actually.

KELSEY: So if you know it could be at any moment, how often are you thinking about eternity? Because if I'm being honest, I can't say I spend much time thinking about Heaven.

KAYLA: It's my favorite part of being a Christian. It's like every fantasy novel I ever read combined into one story,

> but it's real and true and I get to experience it one day.
> Some days I just lay in bed and just try to imagine how
> amazing it will be.

Here are some of her journal entries on the topic. In this first one, she observed the illustration that if you put large rocks (most important things) in your jar (life) first, then you can fit in all the sand (less important things).

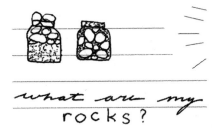

On the next page, she determines what her rocks are: God, family, friends, and school. Then she drew the perspective that *now* is just the *tiniest portion* of eternity, like the beginning of a never ending rope. This picture brings so much joy to my heart!

Kayla challenged herself, knowing that she had a limited amount of time to make a difference in this world.. We can take it as a challenge for ourselves as well.

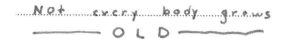

2002 - ? what are you living for? make that dash matter

Our Ultimate Boss Is God

e · t · e · r · n · i · t · y

→ I like the way that looks

f · a · i · t · h

faith

These verses about life beyond this life stood out to her.

8 de enero, 2017   1 Corinthians 3:13
"their work will be shown for what it is, because the Day will bring it to light. It will be revealed with fire, and the fire will test the quality of each person's work.
                        ↑
                eternal intentionality

26 januar, 2017   2 Corinthians 4:18
So we fix our   temporary, but
eyes not on what   what is unseen
is seen, but on   is eternal.
what is unseen,
since what is seen is

19   Titus 1:2a

My   is   raise   by   to   life

aim   to   hopes   pointing   a

without

end.

"My aim is to raise hopes by pointing to a life without end."

∞∞∞∞

The Lord helped Kayla to fix her hope on eternity, and He's using her now to help us do the same.

God, teach us to number our days like Kayla did, that we may gain a heart of wisdom.

She Did Enough

 # victoryoverdeath
 # freedom fromdespair
 # lifethatcounts
 # freshstart
#

Many times, Kayla expressed to me how she wanted to stay young forever and not grow up. This book review is an example of her feelings on this matter.

Anne of ▬

Green Gables

L. M. Montgomery

I *loved* this book! It was full of positivity & whimsy. Anne was a perfect *delight* to read about!

I became so sad when she grew up... as 15 ½ years connect Anne & I (we were around the same age), I wish that she stayed young forever.

Well, Kayla got the desire of her heart!

She didn't live with regrets or wish she was someone else. She was pleased with the life she lived. She stated:

Even if I could travel back in time, I wouldn't because that would change my life and I don't want it to change.

Conversations with Kelsey

As I was just looking through her book, I stumbled upon the section that made me cry more happy tears! It was about a fourteen-year-old who died in a car accident and her memorial service brought so many students to the Lord. It discusses how her going to be with the Lord brought so many to saving faith in Jesus Christ. Sound familiar?

Kayla underlined, "I'll be one of those people who lives to be a history maker at a young age."

I did the math. Kayla lived on this earth 5,866.5 days. Then it got me thinking about this passage in the Bible.

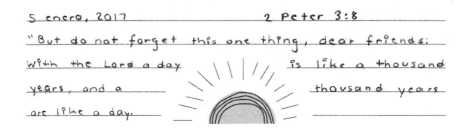

5 enero, 2017   2 Peter 3:8
"But do not forget this one thing, dear friends: With the Lord a day is like a thousand years, and a thousand years are like a day.

There are two ways this verse helps me.

On the one hand, all that Kayla did in her "short" sixteen years gets multiplied in God's realm. To Him, it's like she lived 5,866,500 days. Yep, that's over five million days! All the good she did is exponential!

On the other hand, a thousand years is like a day, so I will see her in the blink of an eye! The time I have remaining until I see her is incredibly short in the scope of eternity. The truth of this brings so much comfort and endurance. It won't be long now.

The phrase I say over and over in my head with joy and relief is "She did enough." It's just true. And she did it with excellence for the glory of her Savior. Jeff and I are so proud of her, and we believe that the Heavenly Father welcomed her home with "Well done, good and faithful servant. You have been faithful over a little; I will set you over much. Enter into the joy of your master." (Matthew 25:23 ESV)

Epilogue

Jesus said, "I am the resurrection and the life. The one who believes in me will live, even though they die; and whoever lives by believing in me will never die. Do you believe this?" (John 11:25-26 NIV). I do. I believe it. Kayla is not dead. She passed from death to life in an instant and did not experience one second without God's presence.

Because she is no longer with us, we mourn, and we miss her so much . . . but we grieve with hope. We focus on how she is more alive than ever and is enjoying Heaven with the One she loves.

Conversations with Kelsey

There's a quote in Francis Chan's book *Crazy Love* that says:

> "If you could have heaven, with no sickness, and with all the friends you ever had on earth, and all the food you ever liked, and all the leisure activities you ever enjoyed, and all the natural beauties you ever saw, all the physi-cal pleasures you ever tasted, and no human conflict or

any natural disasters, could you be satisfied with heaven if Christ were not there?"

My girls and I were discussing that question one Saturday morning at the Coffee Peddlar.

KAYLA: That's not a good question. That doesn't make sense.

KELSEY: Why? (amused at Kayla's bluntness)

KAYLA: It's impossible for any good thing to exist apart from God. He is good, and without Him, nothing can be good. Therefore, *Heaven couldn't have those good things without Christ.*

Do you know if you will join Jesus someday in Heaven?

He said, "What good is it for someone to gain the whole world, yet forfeit their soul?" (Mark 8:36 NIV)

Knowing where your eternal soul will go after your body dies is *the most important issue to settle.*

It is crucial to know that "everyone has sinned; we all fall short of God's glorious standard" (Romans 3:23 NLT). That means all of Kayla's kind actions, generosity, and concern for the world didn't save her. But you might say, "Certainly her good outweighed her bad, right?" Well, yes, in our eyes, but compared to *God's* absolute holiness and perfection, not at all.

My presence requires holiness – because that is who I am   ~ God /\/\/\/\/\/\/\/\/\

> We are all infected and impure with sin. When we display our righteous deeds, they are nothing but filthy rags.
> Isaiah 64:6 NLT

We cannot DRAW NEAR to HPm if we are unclean.
God knows what he's talking about. Do you trust him?

> The Lord looks down from heaven on all mankind to see if there are any who understand, any who seek God. All have turned away, all have become corrupt; there is no one who does good, not even one. Psalm 14:2-3 NIV

Trying to be good doesn't cut it. Following rules and laws doesn't cleanse our hearts, it just shows us how we fall short of a perfect standard. Think about this. Let's say we're out volunteering our time and energy all day long, which is a great thing to do, right? But even one brief jealous thought, bitter feeling, or glance with lust at a person ruins our status before God. It reveals the imperfection of our hearts. We need a cure to permanently change that condition.

All humans have a virus. And it's not called corona. It's called sin. Most people think things like stealing, hatred, and being judgmental are sin. But in reality—these are the *symptoms* of the virus.

The virus is the attitude, "God, I don't need you."

And it can go in various directions, whether you assume "I'll get to Heaven because I'm basically a good person" (i.e. "I can do it on my own") or decide "I don't need God, I want to do my own thing even if it hurts others." *Any* way that doesn't rely on God detaches us from Him. This separation causes shame. Sometimes people try to bury it with addictions or they punish themselves to find relief by using self-harm. People don't know what to do with their guilt.

And this breaks His heart. It could be that the "God" you grew up with doesn't have feelings. But the *true* Heavenly Father *really cares*. He doesn't want you to do life on your own. He loves you and wants a relationship with you. He wants you to let Him in. He wants to heal your broken heart. But He cannot dwell in an infected home. That's why Jesus, His perfect Son, went to the cross. Here's what happened. Read this verse slowly:

> For our sake he made him to be sin who knew no sin, so
> that in him we might become the righteousness of God.
> 2 Corinthians 5:21 ESV

Here's what that means: Jesus took all of your sins, all of my sins, and all the sins of everyone in the whole world on Himself, and he *became* sin so that *sin* died on the cross. To help you understand what this is like, imagine the sweetest dog you know (loyal, loving, obedient). Now imagine it being stalked, attacked, and brutally killed by a pack of wild hyenas. *That* is the horror of what Jesus went through, and he did it *willingly* for His attackers. The Bible calls him "the Lamb of God" because of his precious innocence that was traded for sin. But this is the only way that sin loses its power. It's a shocking trade: Jesus exchanged His righteousness for our sin so we can be free. Only God could be so generous.

This is ultimately how Kayla had no regrets. She relied on the blood of Jesus to cleanse her and make her perfect.

I can't thank God enough that "He has removed our sins as far from us as the east is from the west" (Psalm 103:12 NLT).

But there's even more good news—*He didn't stay dead.* When you think of Jesus, what is the image that dominates your thinking? Is it him on a cross? If so, refocus your thoughts. He is alive! See Him radiant and glorified! He not only conquered sin, He defeated the power of death.

> I am the Living One; I was dead, and now look, I am alive for ever and ever! And I hold the keys of death and Hades. Revelation 1:18 NIV

His resurrection gives us life both now and in eternity. This is how we know that Kayla is alive. This is why we are confident we will see her again. This is how you can too.

> For God so loved the world that he gave his one and only Son, that whoever believes in him shall not perish but have eternal life. For God did not send his Son into the world to condemn the world, but to save the world through him. John 3:16-17 NIV

Do you hear His heart in these two verses? He values us so much that He was willing to pay the maximum price for us!

Jesus wants everyone in his Kingdom.
Repent

If you believe in Him and turn to Him, He will give you freedom! Jesus said, "Those the Father has given me will come to me, and I will never reject them" (John 6:37 NLT).

If you don't have assurance about this, I urge you to give your heart and your life to Jesus. Then your status will be as if you've never sinned. And He will make His home in you until it's time for you to go home to Him—and He will welcome you with open arms.

> Recieve and experience the amazing grace of the Master, Jesus Christ, deep, deep within yourselves.

If you have never done that, and you are ready, you can pray like this:

> God, I want to spend eternity with You. I believe Jesus is your perfect and precious Son who paid the highest price by dying on the cross for me—for my sin of trying to live without You. I need to exchange my sin for Your holiness. I repent of my sin. I renounce my sin. I renounce every power of hell, and I renounce the ways of this world. I surrender my life to You. I am done with living my way, and I am ready to live Your way. I want to know You. Please come into my life. Don't just change me, make me *new*, make me *alive*, replace my heart with Yours right now and forever.

If you prayed that prayer for the first time, you just made the BEST decision of your life! Jesus said, "I tell you the truth, those who listen to my message and believe in God who sent me have eternal life. They will never be condemned for their sins, but they have already passed from death into life" (John 5:24 NLT).

Luke 10:20 : The ultimate prize is your name written in heaven.

Here are some important next steps for you to take:

- Hang out with people who love Jesus. Ask what church they are a part of and get involved. It's important to find a group of people that worships God wholeheartedly.[10]
- Get baptized in water. It's the next step in following Jesus. In the Bible, everyone chose to do this as part of their new commitment to Christ.

> "And now what are you waiting for? Get up, be baptized and wash your sins away, calling on his name." Acts 22:16 NIV

- Read the Bible every day. It's more important than the food you eat! The Gospel of John is a great place to start. You can download the YouVersion Bible App for those who don't yet have a paper Bible. The New Living Translation is an easier one to understand. Read a chapter each day. It's how you will get to know Jesus.

> "Now this is eternal life: that they know you, the only true God, and Jesus Christ, whom you have sent." John 17:3 NIV

---

[10] This website can be a good starting place to help you find a church family. **bit.ly/helpmefindachurch**

- Start talking to God about everything. This is prayer, and it's your lifeline.

  > But when you pray, go away by yourself, shut the door behind you, and pray to your Father in private. Then your Father, who sees everything, will reward you. Matthew 6:6 NLT

- Ask God to fill you with His powerful Holy Spirit so you can boldly tell others this good news and bring His Kingdom everywhere you go. Don't try to do it on your own. Rely on the Spirit of Jesus.

All who believe in Christ have a secure hope for a glorious future. Here is the promise of what is to come:

> He will wipe every tear from their eyes. There will be no more death or mourning or crying or pain, for the old order of things has passed away. He who was seated on the throne said, "I am making everything new!" Then he said, "Write this down, for these words are trustworthy and true." Revelation 21:4-5 NIV

We will have new resurrected bodies that never get sick and die. We will be free from everything that depresses us. There will be no more injustice, no more loneliness, heartache, or loss. We will live together in perfect relationships. And best of all, we get to be with Jesus, the one who made it all possible.

Dear friends, now we are children of God, and what we will be has not yet been made known. But we know that when Christ appears, we shall be like him, for we shall see him as he is.
1 John 3:2 NIV

I want you to know that you are loved, valued, and cherished. I hope to meet you here or on the other side. Thank you for reading about the girl who had no regrets. May it be true of you, too!

all of
heaven
is cheering
YOU
on

Ways to Connect

Email: KaylaDbook@gmail.com

Facebook: She Had No Regrets

Instagram: @she_had_no_regrets

Society6 (her artwork collections): bit.ly/SkyeMarie

Fine Art America (my artwork): bit.ly/JuliaKayArt

Acknowledgments

Father in Heaven, I praise and thank You for all You've done. Everything good comes from You!

Thank you for:

- blessing me with a wonderful, supportive husband, and two precious daughters.
- saving Kayla and surrounding her with amazing friends, family, teachers, and leaders.
- calling me to write even though I felt unqualified and bringing greater measures of healing to my soul as I obeyed.
- giving Rachel understanding and patience as I stood at my computer for hours every day.
- my cherished sister, Cindy, whom You gifted with strong editing skills and a loving heart.
- the generous provision of those dear ones who saw the vision for this book and wanted to see it published and distributed.
- the design team that did a beautiful job and the book packaging team, especially Chad Harrington who valued our daughter even while suffering his own loss.

God, I ask you to bless each person *above and beyond all that they could ask or imagine*. Refill them for all they poured out. In Jesus' name, Amen.

> Give, and you will receive. Your gift will return to you in full—pressed down, shaken together to make room for more, running over, and poured into your lap . . . Luke 6:38 NLT

About the Author

JULIA KAY DUERLER comes from a long line of Christ-followers. She chose to trust in Jesus when she was six-years-old, knowing even then that she needed a Savior. As a young teen, she started to veer from His path, but He recaptured her heart before her freshman year of high school. The best choice she ever made was to dedicate her entire life to Him. She has been on a path of following Jesus ever since. He led her to get a B.S. in Family and Children's Ministry from Toccoa Falls College, then an N.D. from Trinity College of Natural Health. Julia most values her "MRS. degree" in marriage to Jeff and her "MOM degree" in raising Kayla and Rachel. She directs the Restorative Prayer ministry at LifeSpring and enjoys creating fine art and decent meals. More than anything, she wants the world to know that God is a good and powerful God. His joy is her strength!

Made in the USA
Columbia, SC
08 August 2020